Gilbert Simondon an

MW01088047

Technologies of Lived Abstraction
Brian Massumi and Erin Manning, editors

Gilbert Simondon and the Philosophy of the Transindividual

Muriel Combes

translated, with preface and afterword, by Thomas LaMarre

The MIT Press
Cambridge, Massachusetts
London, England

Originally published as *Simondon, Individu et collectivité*, by Muriel Combes. © Presses Universitaires de France, 1999

MIT Press books may be purchased at special quantity discounts for business or sales promotional use. For information, please email special_sales@mitpress.mit.edu or write to Special Sales Department, The MIT Press, 55 Hayward Street, Cambridge, MA 02142.

This book was set in Stone Sans and Stone Serif by the MIT Press. Printed and bound in the United States of America.

Library of Congress Cataloging-in-Publication Data

Combes, Muriel, 1971–.
[Simondon. English]
Gilbert Simondon and the philosophy of the transindividual / Muriel Combes ; translated, with preface and afterword, by Thomas LaMarre.
    p. cm.—(Technologies of lived abstraction)
Includes bibliographical references.
ISBN 978-0-262-01818-0 (hardcover : alk. paper), 978-0-262-53747-6 (pb.)
1. Simondon, Gilbert. 2. Individuation (Philosophy). I. Title.
B2430.S554C6613   2013
194—dc23
2012013224

10 9 8 7 6 5 4 3

To Titus

Contents

Abbreviations

IG	*L'individu et sa genèse physico-biologique*, Presses Universitaires de France, 1964; Éditions Jérôme Millon, 1995.
IPC	*L'individuation psychique et collective*, Aubier, 1989.
IL	*L'individuation à la lumière des notions de forme et d'information*, Éditions Jérôme Millon, 2005.
MEOT	*Du mode d'existence des objets techniques*, Aubier, 1958, 1969, 1989.

Trans. note: At the time when Combes was writing, the complete collected edition of Simondon's work on individuation, *L'individuation à la lumière des notions de forme et d'information*, had not been published. Because this edition is now the standard, throughout the text I have added page references to it (*IL*) following Combes's references to the prior editions (*IG* and *IPC*).

Series Foreword

"What moves as a body, returns as the movement of thought."

Of subjectivity (in its nascent state)
Of the social (in its mutant state)
Of the environment (at the point it can be reinvented)

"A process set up anywhere reverberates everywhere."

The Technologies of Lived Abstraction book series is dedicated to work of transdisciplinary reach inquiring critically but especially creatively into processes of subjective, social, and ethical-political emergence abroad in the world today. Thought and body, abstract and concrete, local and global, individual and collective: the works presented are not content to rest with the habitual divisions. They explore how these facets come formatively, reverberatively together, if only to form the movement by which they come again to differ.

Possible paradigms are many: autonomization, relation; emergence, complexity, process; individuation, (auto)poiesis; direct perception, embodied perception, perception-as-action; speculative pragmatism, speculative realism, radical empiricism; mediation, virtualization; ecology of practices, media ecology; technicity; micropolitics, biopolitics, ontopower. Yet there will be a common aim: to catch new thought and action dawning, at a creative crossing. The Technologies of Lived Abstraction series orients to the creativity at this crossing, in virtue of which life everywhere can be considered germinally aesthetic, and the aesthetic anywhere already political.

"Concepts must be experienced. They are lived."

—Erin Manning and Brian Massumi

Preface

Thomas LaMarre

Published in 1999, Muriel Combes's introduction to the work of Gilbert Simondon ushered in a new era of serious engagement with his thinking *as philosophy*. Oddly enough, although Simondon's first book, *Du mode d'existence des objets techniques* (On the mode of existence of technical objects, 1958), won him instant acclaim, his second book, *L'individu et sa genèse physico-biologique* (The individual and its physico-biological genesis, 1964) met with considerably less enthusiasm. The first book had so thoroughly established the image of Simondon as a "thinker of technics" that readers subsequently could not bridge the gap between the first book on technics and the second book, so clearly philosophical, on individuation, even though both works were extensions of his doctoral theses. In fact, the sense of a gap between the two projects remained so profound that there was no call to publish the second part of Simondon's philosophy of individuation, *L'individuation psychique et collective* (Psychic and collective individuation) until 1989. In effect, until 1989, Simondon's philosophy of individuation was not generally accessible.

The publication of *L'individuation psychique et collective* renewed interest in Simondon's work, and the 1990s saw a number of efforts to bridge the gap that reception of his work had introduced between his thinking on technics and his philosophy of individuation: an international conference was held in 1992, the proceedings of which were subsequently published under the title *Gilbert Simondon: Une pensée de l'individuation et de la technique*, which clearly signals the central task: thinking his philosophy of individuation *and* of technics. Two participants in that conference would later publish books on Simondon: Gilbert Hottois published the first general introduction to his philosophy in 1993 under the title *Simondon et la philosophie de la "culture technique"* (Simondon and the philosophy of technical culture), and in his three-volume work entitled *Time and Technics* (1994, 1996, 2001), Bernard Stiegler gives a prominent position to Simondon. Interest in his work increased gradually to the point where Simondon's philosophy of individuation has finally been published in a single volume, *L'individuation à la lumière des notions de forme et d'information* (Individuation in light of notions of form and information, 2005), and no fewer than three special issues of journals dedicated to his work have appeared in recent years—*Multitudes* (2005), *Parrhesia* (2009), *Inflexions* (2012)—with essays by a broad range of contemporary thinkers—Didier Debaise, Bruno Latour, Brian Massumi, Antonio Negri, Isabelle Stengers, and Alberto Toscano, among others.

Significantly, Muriel Combes's presentation of Simondon frequently figures as an essential point of reference in these recent evaluations of his philosophy. There are several reasons that Combes's succinct introduction has played such a pivotal role. First, she sets herself the task of bridging the gap between Simondon's account of technics and his philosophy of individuation, but rather than starting with the relation between technics and individuation, she turns to the postulates of his philosophy, leaving an account of technics for the last chapter. In the early chapters of the book, she avoids familiar terms and notions that, if used as a point of departure, introduce hierarchies and distinctions into thought that are not at all in keeping with Simondon's philosophy as a whole. Especially problematic are the notions of culture, technics, norm, nature, majority, the human. Many analyses have stumbled and fallen over such notions, for, if taken at face value, they push thought into dualism and substantialism, undermining the systemic movement of Simondon's thinking, while thrusting aside such key concepts as preindividual, value, genealogy, operation, and individuation itself, as well as the central postulate of the reality of relation. By carefully laying out the ground for Simondon's philosophy, Combes succeeds in transforming our understanding of fundamental questions of culture and technics, while renewing the philosophy of nature and of technology.

Second, where other commentators have often ignored Simondon's meticulous articulation of orders of gradation and consequently have fallen back on foundations and normative distinctions, Combes truly sticks with the complexity that arises from his central postulates, not only adhering to the reality and operativity of relation at the heart of Simondon's strategic reconsideration of epistemology and ontology, but also tracing his basic paradigm for individuation across physical, natural, and technical beings, and exploring how Simondon's thinking unfolds across orders of complexity: affect, emotion, perception, knowledge, and action.

Third, in highlighting the significance of labor as a pivotal issue in Simondon's politics of technics, Combes underscores the political implications of the philosophy of individuation in a manner that proves quite prescient. Although Simondon's theory of information has nothing in common with information theory in the usual sense of transmitted data (or in the cybernetic sense, for that matter), the danger remains that his emphasis on networks, information, and reticularity will be taken not as a potential critique of contemporary technical networks but as an instantiation of them. To wit, we would not really need Simondon because the present is already Simondonian. Drawing on Antonio Negri and what is sometimes called postoperaism, Combes astutely situates what is at stake in new ways of thinking about process (individuation) and structure (individual), and the transformations of the one into the other. She makes clear the stakes of beginning at the level of the ontological and epistemological to ground a discussion of the technopolitical. Thus she asks: If we do not assume that the knowledge of factory workers vis-à-vis machines is necessarily servile (as Simondon sometimes appears to do), how may we learn from the perspective of those who work with machines? Within Combes's particular focus on factory labor, a broader question lurks that is true to Simondon's concerns: *What would a nonservile knowledge of technics look like today?* What can it do, and how can nonservile thought be amplified in action? Because Combes focuses on the effort to articulate a nonservile relation to technology at the heart of Simondon's philosophy, she succeeds in showing the relevance of his approach beyond the limits that he himself sometimes places on it, and despite her disagreement with some aspects of his evaluation of particular situations.

Nonetheless, the power of Combes's account does not lie merely in a take-home message. Her style of writing enacts her manner of thinking. In this respect, her notes and passing remarks on grammar and punctuation, which might slip by unnoticed, afford a clue to what it means to write processually. For instance, in her note on Simondon's style in chapter 1, Combes remarks that, because the French language does not afford conjugations like the gerund -*ing* that in English may serve to foreground processes, as in, for example, what is happen*ing*, Simondon has to invent a style: "For all its subtlety, this style is nonetheless tangible, relying in large part on a specific usage of punctuation: it is thus not rare to see deployed, in a phrase composed of brief propositions connected with semicolons, all the phases of a movement of being or of an emotion." The same is true of Combes's style, and it became all the more tangible for me in the process of translating, because, in addition to what may initially appear to be an unwarranted overuse of semicolons, Combes is so fond of qualified phrases and relative clauses that simple declarative sentences appear utterly disqualified. How are we to understand such a style?

If we wish to understand the conceptual flow of such a style, we have to resist two tendencies of stylistic interpretation. On the one hand, we must resist the tendency to attribute such twists and turns to academic habits of thought in the sense of a deliberate obliqueness and complexity designed to render esoteric even the simplest observation. For all that thought or philosophy, like any tradition and discipline, entails concerns and forms of expression that may prove difficult, such concerns constitute a threshold of understanding, not a deliberate barrier to it, and in this respect, Combes's text is an exemplar of clarity and cogency—not despite the twists and turns of her style but because of them.

On the other hand, even though Combes refers us to differences between standardized national languages (for lack of a better term) such as French and English, we should not for all that reify the unities of national language, and conclude that her style is merely a reflection or manifestation of the French language. Combes is abundantly aware of the distinctions running through her language, and carefully delineates prepositional phrases. For instance: "From a lexical point of view, this opposition between *à travers* ("through" or "by way of") and *à partir de* ("from" or "on the basis of") expresses the great distance separating processual thought from foundational thought." Similarly, she consistently calls attention to conceptual distinctions in terminology, such as Simondon's use of *rapport* (relationship) to refer to the process of linking already individuated terms, while *relation* (relation) is associated with individuation itself. In other words, Combes is very attentive to differences within an apparently unified and settled language, but such difference is not deployed deconstructively; that is to say, it is not used rhetorically to displace an initial determination in a process of infinite regression. This is because, as the above examples indicate, Combes addresses language not as grammar but as a matter of modalities. And so, in a manner that is necessarily idiosyncratic and disciplined at the same time, Combes builds on distinctions or determinations in a movement of complication. It is through an exploration of the *relationship* between already individuated terms (received conceptual distinctions) that Combes manages simultaneously to "work the *relation*," that is, to follow and complicate the individuation underlying the individuated terms, operatively.

In effect, then, in Combes's insistent use of semicolons, relative clauses, and interlinear qualifications, we can read precisely the virtues she attributes to Simondon's style: We glean all the phases of a movement of being or of a concept. Put another way, and to cite from another of Combes's provocative notes, hers is a style rejecting "the substantialist approach that believes itself capable of defining the object independently of the predicates that can be attributed to it." As such, thinking individuation in the act of writing is not a matter of adding predications to an object or subject. Rather, writing becomes a process of predicating, through which objects and subjects become individuated. Such writing is not only a matter of an inversion that makes objects transitive to their sensible qualities, for the subject is not given in advance, either. This act of predicating is not a matter of transitive or intransitive, but of both: in the mode of the transductive.

In translating Combes's text, fidelity to such a style becomes difficult. This is partly because the use of gender in French affords distinctions that drop out in English. For instance, the overall orientation for a series of relative clauses and qualifications remains clear in French because we know that "elle" refers to "la relation," and "il" or "lui" to "le rapport." In English translation, however, the result is a long sentence populated with numerous instances of "its" where we lose all sense of which "it" is in play. While such an effect is not without interest, it runs counter to Combes's style, which complicates determinations and orientations, building upon a layering of orientations, rather than simply blurring and confusing them. Consequently, instead of confusing matters with sentences stringing together "it" after "it," I have often repeated nouns as a point of reference. Likewise, in a few instances, some sentences proved unwieldy in English, and I opted for a series of shorter phrases. In addition, when it comes to transitions, one of Combes's favorite gestures is to begin a sentence with "for" (*car*), as if it were the cause for the prior sentence, yet such causality does not prove to be linear, for the sentences are in fact predicating one other. Such an effect does not obtain directly in English, and so I adopted a series of other strategies to indicate something of the weird causality of predication between sentences.

On the whole, however, I took care to follow her style rather literally, even when it may appear needlessly complicated in English, because there is indeed a processual logic to her style that, in my opinion, contributes to the success of her presentation. Indeed, her writing affords a deeper confrontation with the modalities of language, especially at the level of the so-called reflexive verb forms in French that can go in so many different directions in English translation, sometimes becoming intransitive (*s'individuer* becomes to "individuate"), sometimes remaining reflexive (*se trouver* becomes "to find itself"), sometimes becoming flattened (*se trouver* becomes "to be [located]"), or turning passive (*se dire* becomes "to be said"). Such a concern in the act of translating so-called reflexive verbs actually enacts a key process in Simondon's and Combes's manners of thinking: what may appear from the perspective of the subject as reflexive or even intransitive (thus grounding the sense of a disembodied subject) turns out, in fact, from the perspective of individuation and the relation, to be transductive, an actual being, an actually encephalized body. And it is in that sense that my translation of Combes–Simondon strives to enact a transductive relation called the transindividual.

Translator's Acknowledgments

Special thanks to Brian Massumi and Erin Manning, for their brilliant comments and encouragement; to Andrew Goffey, for his insightful suggestions on the translation; to Marie-Pier Boucher and Patrick Harrop, who organized the initial workshop on Simondon in Montreal in conjunction with Erin Manning's Sense Lab; and to Felix Rebolledo, Charles Gagnon, and Patrick Harrop, whose work on an English translation of *Du mode d'existence des objets techniques* spurred deeper engagement with issues of translation in the context of the workshop.

Introduction

To date, only three works by Gilbert Simondon have been published. Two of them come from his doctoral thesis, defended in 1958 and published in two volumes twenty-five years apart: *L'individu et sa genèse physico-biologique* (The individual and its physico-biological genesis [*IG*], 1964) and *L'individuation psychique et collective* (Psychic and collective individuation [*IPC*], 1989). For many readers, however, Simondon's name is associated with *Du mode d'existence des objets techniques* (On the mode of existence of technical objects [*MEOT*], 1958), a work that brought him into the public eye in the same year in which he defended his thesis on individuation.

As a consequence, Simondon was greeted as a "thinker of technics" rather than as a philosopher whose ambitions lay in an in-depth renewal of ontology. Rather than invited to philosophy conferences, he was most frequently cited in pedagogical reports on teaching technology. He did, in fact, devote most of his life to teaching, notably in the general psychology and technology laboratory that he founded at the University of Paris V, and his work on technics often adopts an explicitly pedagogical point of view.

Even those who saw in his philosophy of individuation a way to renew metaphysics, paying him homage in this capacity, have nonetheless treated him more as a *source of inspiration* than an *essential reference*. Gilles Deleuze is an exception to the silence that has greeted Simondon's work, explicitly citing *L'individu et sa genèse physico-biologique* in *The Logic of Sense* and in *Difference and Repetition* as early as 1969. Deleuze also marks the beginning of new lines of inquiry—not always philosophical—that tend to prolong Simondon's thought rather than explicate it. Deleuze and Guattari's *A Thousand Plateaus* draws a great deal more from Simondon's works than it cites from them. And a philosopher of science like Isabelle Stengers, as well as sociologists and psychologists of labor, such as Marcelle Stroobants, Philippe Zarifian, and Yves Clot, bring Simondon's hypotheses into play within their respective fields of research.

I wish here to explore an aspect of Simondon's thought avoided by the handful of commentaries sparked by his work, namely, an outline of an ethics and politics adequate to the hypothesis of preindividual being. These ethics and politics come to the fore in the concept of transindividual, which I attempt to use as a point of view on the theory of individuation as a whole.

Distancing Simondon from his identity as the "thinker of technics" is a necessary condition for pursuing his line of inquiry on the collective, which will draw reserves of transformation from the sources of affectivity. Such an approach also allows us to discover something other than cultural pedagogy in his work on technics. From preindividual to transindividual by way of a renewal of the philosophy of relation—this is but one pathway within Simondon's philosophy. It is the one that I take here.

On Being and the Status of the One: From the Relativity of the Real to the Reality of Relation

The Operation

It is possible to read all of Simondon's work as a call for a transmutation in how we approach being. Pursued across physical, biological, psycho-social, and technological domains, this exploration of being assumes a "reformation of our understanding," especially of our philosophical under-standing. Expounded in detail in the introduction to *L'individu et sa genèse physico-biologique*, the gesture authorizing Simondon's reflection as a whole receives a definitive formulation at the end of the introduction. Simondon explains that being is used in two senses, which are generally confused. On the one hand, "being is being as such," which is to say, there is being, about which we can initially only confirm its "givenness."[1] On the other hand, "being is being insofar as it is individuated." This latter sense of being, in which being appears as a multiplicity of individual beings, is "always superimposed upon the former sense within the theory of logic" (*IG*, 34; *IL*, 36). Although this criticism seems specific to logic, it applies, in fact, to the entire philosophical tradition, which perpetuates this confusion. Just as logic deals with statements that are relative to being after individuation, so philosophy focuses on being as individuated, thus conflating being with individuated being.

   In this respect, the philosophical tradition boils down to two tenden-cies, both of which are blind to the reality of being *before* all individuation: atomism and hylomorphism.[2] The common reproach addressed to these two doctrines is that they think being on the model of the One and thus, at some level, assume the existence of the individual they seek to account for. This is where the greatest errors of the entire philosophical tradition are compounded, which makes the problem of individuation the central prob-lem of philosophy for the author of *L'individu et sa genèse physico-biologique*. The philosophical tradition deals with the problem of individuation entirely *on the basis of* the individual. As a consequence, it stubbornly wishes to disclose a *principle of individuation*, which it can only think in the form of a *term* that is already given. Thus the atomism of Epicurus and Lucretius posits the atom as primary substantial reality that, owing to the miraculous event of the clinamen, deviates from its trajectory and enters into assemblies with other atoms to form an individual; or likewise, hylomorphism makes the individual the result of an encounter between form and matter that are always already individuated: thus Thomas of Aquinas situates the principle of individuation in matter, which in his opinion allows for the individuation of creatures within a species. In Simondon's view, hylomorphism and atomism seek to explain the result of individuation by a principle of the same nature, which leads them to think being in the form of the individual. But a philosophy that truly wishes to address individuation must separate what tradition has always conflated, to *distinguish being as such from being as individual*. In such a perspective, being as such is necessarily understood in terms of the gap separating it from individuated being. And by the same token, we can no longer remain content to confirm the "givenness" of being but would have to specify what properly characterizes "being as such," which is not only its being but also its not being *one*. In Simondon's thought, being as being is not one, because it precedes any individual. This is why he calls it *preindividual*.

To understand the passage from preindividual being to individuated being, we must not embark on a search for a principle of individuation. This is where traditional ontology has gone astray: in privileging the constituted term, it has ignored the *operation* constituting the individual, that is, *individuation as process*. To understand individuation, we must turn to the process wherein a principle is not only put to work but also constituted. With this initial gesture of disentangling being as such and being as individual, Simondon substitutes individuation for the individual, and operation for principle. The result is what we might call a first "order-word," a first requirement for thought: "seek to know the individual through individuation rather than individuation through the individual" (*IG*, 22; *IL*, 24). The individual is thus neither the source nor the term of inquiry but merely the result of an operation of individuation. This is why the genesis of the individual remains a question for philosophy only as a moment in a becoming of being, a becoming that sweeps it along. When we retrace the genesis of physical and biological individuals or of psychic and collective reality, we always focus on the becoming of being, precisely because it is being that is individuated. As such, being can be adequately known only from its middle, by seizing it at its center (*by way of* the operation of individuation and

not *on the basis of* the term of this operation).[3] Simondon's approach entails
a substitution of ontogenesis for traditional ontology, grasping the genesis
of individuals within the operation of individuation as it is unfolding.

More-Than-One

The source of all individuals, preindividual being, is not *one*. Which immediately poses the question: How should we think this being that is individuating, which, as a consequence, cannot take the form of *an* individual?
If it is true that "unity and identity are only applicable to one of the phases
of being, subsequent to the operation of individuation" (*IG*, 23; *IL*, 25–26),
and if, as a consequence, being before individuation—that is, being as
such—is not one, then what are we to make of it? How are we to understand the existence of individuated beings on the basis of this being that
is not one?

Posed in this manner, the question is not entirely adequate; and it would
be an unfortunate approximation for us to suppose that, because being is
not one, it is *not-one*. Properly speaking, we would have to say that being
is more-than-one, which is to say, it "can be taken as more-than-unity
and more-than-identity" (*IG*, 30; *IL*, 32). In such enigmatic expressions as
"more-than-unity" and "more-than-identity," we see coming to light the
idea whereby being is constitutively, immediately, a power of mutation. In
fact, the non-self-identity of being is not simply a passage from one identity
to another through the negation of the prior identity. Rather, because being
contains potential, and because all that is exists with a reserve of becoming,
the non-self-identity of being should be called *more*-than-identity. In this
sense, being is *in excess* over itself. And to clarify this description of being,
Simondon borrows a series of notions from thermodynamics. Thinking preindividual being as a system that is neither stable nor instable demands
recourse to the notion of *metastability*.

A physical system is said to be in metastable equilibrium (or false equilibrium) when the least modification of system parameters (pressure, temperature, etc.) suffices to break its equilibrium. Thus, in super-cooled water (i.e.,
water remaining liquid at a temperature below its freezing point), the least
impurity with a structure isomorphic to that of ice plays the role of a seed for
crystallization and suffices to turn the water to ice. Before all individuation,
being can be understood as a system containing potential energy. Although
this energy becomes active within the system, it is called potential because
it requires a transformation of the system in order to be structured, that is,
to be actualized in accordance with structures. Preindividual being, and in

a general way, any system in a metastable state, harbors potentials that are incompatible because they belong to heterogeneous dimensions of being. This is why preindividual being can be perpetuated only by *dephasing*. The notion of dephasing, which in thermodynamics indicates a change in state of a system, becomes the term for becoming in Simondon's philosophy. Being is becoming, and becoming happens in phases. But dephasing is prior to phases, which stem from it—this is why preindividual being can be said to be without phase. Still, a phase is neither a simple appearance relative to an observer (phases of the moon) nor a temporal movement destined to be replaced by another (a dialectical movement of becoming, as Hegel conceives of it, for instance), but an "aspect that is the result of a doubling of being" (*MEOT*, 159), which is relative to other aspects resulting from other individuations. Thermodynamics teaches us that a system changing state (e.g., water evaporating or turning to ice) contains two subsystems or two phases (liquid and gas or liquid and solid) that it brings together. If we describe being as a system in the process of becoming, we will then conclude that it is necessarily polyphased.

The emergence of an individual within preindividual being should be conceived in terms of the resolution of a tension between potentials belonging to previously separated orders of magnitude. A plant, for instance, establishes communication between a cosmic order (that to which the energy of light belongs) and an inframolecular order (that of mineral salts, oxygen, etc.). But the individuation of a plant does not only give birth to the plant in question. In dephasing, being always simultaneously gives birth to an individual mediating two orders of magnitude *and* to a milieu at the same level of being (thus the milieu of the plant will be the earth on which it is located and the immediate environment with which it interacts). No individual would be able to exist without a milieu that is its complement, arising simultaneously from the operation of individuation: for this reason, the individual should be seen as but a partial result of the operation bringing it forth. Thus, in a general manner, we may consider individuals as beings that come into existence as so many partial solutions to so many problems of incompatibility between separate levels of being. And it is owing to tension and incompatibility between potentials harbored within the preindividual that being dephases or becomes, in order to perpetuate itself. Becoming, here, does not affect the being from the outside, as an accident affects a substance, but constitutes one of its dimensions. Being only is in becoming, that is, by its structuring in diverse domains of individuation (physical, biological, psychosocial, and also, in a certain sense, technological) through the work of operations.

It is only possible to think the formation of individuated beings if we think of them as a function of preindividual being understood as "more-than-one," that is, as a metastable system laden with potentials. But being is not exhausted in the individuals that it becomes. In each phase of its becoming, it remains more-than-one. "Being as being is entirely given in each of its phases, but with a reserve of becoming" (*IG*, 229; *IL*, 317). To think this reserve of becoming, this preindividual charge that resides in these partially individuated systems, and to arrive at a new understanding of the production of the relationship between being and being one, Simondon will round off his borrowings from thermodynamics with a cybernetic inspiration. In particular, he will replace "notions of substance, form, and matter," which are inadequate for thinking the operation whereby being comes to be individuated, "with more fundamental notions of primary information, internal resonance, potential energy, and orders of magnitude" (*IG*, 30; *IL*, 32). Nonetheless, the traditional notions are not so much dismissed as revised. Those of form and matter are now connected to an understanding of being as a system in tension, and are seen as operators of a process rather than as the final terms of an operation consigned to the shadows. Form, in particular, ceases to be understood as a principle of individuation acting on matter from without, becoming *information*. In this new conceptual context, information loses the sense conferred on it by the technology of transmissions (which thinks of it as what circulates between an emitter and a receiver), to designate the very operation of taking on form, the irreversible direction in which individuation operates. The example of the process of molding a brick from clay clarifies especially well this renewal of notions for describing individuation (*IG*, 37–49; *IL*, 39–51). Aware of the paradigmatic value of this example, Simondon completely discredits a hylomorphic reading of it. Because hylomorphism sees in molding only the imposition of a form upon matter, it retains of the process only its final terms (i.e., form and matter), obscuring the important point, the operation of taking on form itself. Now, the clay matter and the parallelepipedic form of the mold are only endpoints of two technological half-trajectories, of two half-chains that, upon being joined, make for the individuation of the clay brick. Such individuation is *modulation*, in which "matter and form are made present as forces" (*IG*, 42; *IL*, 44). Clay is not informed by the mold from without: it is potential for deformations; it harbors within it a positive property that allows it to be deformed, such that the mold acts as a limit imposed on these deformations. Pursuing this schema, we would say that it is the clay itself that "takes form in accordance with the mold" (*IG*,43; *IL*, 45). Matter is never naked matter, any more than form is pure; rather, it is as a materialized form that the mold can act on matter that has been prepared, that has the capacity to conduct the worker's energy from point to point, molecule by molecule. The clay can eventually be transformed into bricks because it possesses colloidal properties that render it capable of conducting a deforming energy while maintaining the coherence of molecular chains, because it is in a sense "already in form" in the swampy earth. In such a description, the individuation of a clay brick appears as an evolving energetic system, which is very different from how hylomorphism sees it, as a relation between two terms that are alien to one another.

Reconsidered as a metastable system, being before all individuation is a field rich in potentials that can only *be* by *becoming*, that is, by individuating. Preindividual being is richer than mere self-identity because it has what it takes to become. Also, as we have seen, preindividual being is more-than-one: does this mean that it has no unity of any kind?

Transduction

Being "does not possess unity of identity which is that of the stable state in which no transformation is possible: being possesses transductive unity" (*IG*, 29; *IL*, 31). That being is more-than-unity does not mean that there is never any unity: rather, it means that being one occurs within being, and must be understood as a relative store of the "spacing out of being," of its capacity for dephasing. We will call this mode of unity of being, across its diverse phases and multiple individuations, *transduction*. This is Simondon's second gesture. It consists in elaborating this unique notion of transduction, which results in a specific method and ultimately in an entirely new way of envisioning the mode of relation obtaining between thought and being.

Transduction is first defined as the operation whereby a domain undergoes *information*—in the sense that Simondon gives to this term, which we have discussed in the example of molding a brick: "By transduction, we mean a physical, biological, mental, or social operation, through which an activity propagates from point to point within a domain, while grounding this propagation in the structuration of the domain, which is operated from place to place: each region of the constituted structure serves as a principle of constitution for the next region" (*IG*, 30; *IL*, 32). The clearest image of this operation, according to Simondon, is that of the crystal that, from a very small seed, grows in all directions within its aqueous solution, wherein "each molecular layer already constituted serves as a structuring base for the layer in the process of forming" (*IG*, 31; *IL*, 33). Transduction expresses the processual sense of individuation; this is why it holds for any domain, and the determination of domains (matter, life, mind, society) relies on diverse regimes of individuation (physical, biological, psychic, collective).

Simondon's gesture of understanding individuation as an individuating operation has profound methodological and ontological consequences. In particular, theories of knowledge inspired by Kant, in which the possibility of knowledge is grounded in the constituting activity of the knowing subject, are shattered. To begin with the operation of individuation is to place oneself at the level of the polarization of a preindividual dyad (formed by an energetic condition and a structural seed). The preindividual dyad is prenoetic as well, which is to say, it precedes both thought and individual. And thought itself is nothing more than one of the phases of being-becoming, *because the operation of individuation does not admit of an already constituted observer*. The transductive constitution of beings itself requires a transductive description. This is why Simondon also calls *transduction* a "procedure of the mind as it discovers. This procedure consists in *following being in its genesis*, in carrying out the genesis of thought at the same time as the genesis of the object is carried out" (*IG*, 32; *IL*, 34). Contrary to the goal Kant assigns the theory of knowledge, it is not here a matter of defining the conditions of *possibility* and the limits of knowledge, but rather of thought accompanying the *real* constitution of individuated beings. The object of knowledge appears only upon the stabilization of the operation of individuation, when the operation, incorporated into its result, disappears. In this inevitable "veiling" of the constituting operation by its constituted result, Simondon finds the cause for the forgetting of the operation, which is characteristic of the philosophical tradition. Philosophy, having forgotten to take into account the operation of the real constitution of individuals, thus focuses its attention on the ideal constitution of the object of knowledge.

To resolve the problem of knowledge, working against the Kantian hylomorphism that separates a priori forms from the sensibility of matter given a posteriori, Simondon situates himself before the rupture between the object to be known and the subject of knowledge. Indeed, in his view, knowledge is not grounded on the side of the subject any more than it is on the side of the object. As he writes in *L'individuation psychique et collective*: "If knowledge rediscovers the lines that allow for interpreting the world according to stable laws, it is not because there exist in the subject a priori forms of sensibility, whose coherence with brute facts coming from the world would be inexplicable; it is because being as subject and being as object arise from the same primitive reality, and the thought that now appears to institute an inexplicable relation between object and subject in fact prolongs this initial individuation; the *conditions of possibility* of knowledge are in fact the *causes of existence* of the individuated being" (*IPC*, 127; *IL*, 264). Thus, with a single gesture, Simondon steers clear of subjectivism as well as objectivism, for the study of the conditions of possibility of knowledge follows from the problem of the genesis of being. Still, if he criticizes the theory of knowledge, it is in order to shift the stakes: from the perspective of a philosophy of individuation, *one can only account for the possibility of knowing individuated beings by providing a description of their individuation.* And because "the existence of the individuated being as subject is anterior to knowledge" (*IPC*, 163; *IL*, 284), the problem of the conditions of possibility for knowledge is resolved within the ontogenesis of the subject. As Simondon writes, "we cannot, in the habitual sense of the term, *know individuation*; we can only individuate, individuating ourselves, and individuating within ourselves" (*IG*, 34; *IL*, 36). The knowledge of individuation—although surely it would be better to speak here of description rather than knowledge—presupposes an individuation of knowledge: "Beings can be known through the subject's knowledge, but the individuation of beings can only be grasped through the individuation of the subject's knowledge" (*IG*, 34; *IL*, 36). Consequently, the problem of grounding knowledge is canceled out. The traditional problematic of the conditions of knowledge proves useless: because traditional logic is only interested in terms, it is powerless to describe the self-production of being. And the notion of transduction thus comes to designate another model of thought, adequate from the genetic point of view.

As he works out his notion of transduction, Simondon "transgresses" the Kantian limits on reason. In transduction, metaphysics and logic merge: "it expresses individuation and allows it to be thought; . . . *it applies to ontogenesis and is ontogenesis itself*" (*IG*, 31; *IL*, 33). Such an approach appears to offer a reinterpretation of the thesis of Parmenides, wherein "The same, itself, is at once thinking and being":[4] that thinking and being are "the same" means that what constitutes thought is not different from what constitutes being; thought and being are only adequately grasped when their transductive dimension is grasped: the ground of thought and of being is transduction. One of the effects of the problematic of individuation is thus to reconfigure the "relationship" between thinking and being. Both ideas and beings stem from individuating operations, which may be said to be parallel, for the knowledge of individuation is "an operation parallel to the operation known" (*IG*, 34; *IL*, 36). This reconfiguration of the relationship between thinking and being is comparable to that which Spinoza brings into play around the notion of power. Spinozan substance, defined by an infinity of attributes (of which only two, extension and thought, are accessible to our understanding), has two powers: a power of existing and acting (defined by the infinity of its attributes) and a power of thinking everything that it brings into existence (which the attribute that is thought, profiting in this perspective from a privilege of redoubling, succeeds in filling—there are ideas of ideas). Being and thinking in Spinoza are two powers of substance, much as they are two "sides" of individuation in Simondon.[5]

With the notion of transduction, Simondon thus displaces the traditional line of inquiry: for the problem of the possibility of knowledge, he substitutes that of individuation of knowledge. Now, he tells us, it is a matter of an analogical operation: "Individuation between the real exterior and the subject is grasped by the subject due to the analogical individuation of knowledge in the subject" (*IG*, 34; *IL*, 36). It follows that what now guarantees the legitimacy of the method, that is, the adequacy of the description to reality, is the analogical and self-grounded dimension of the procedure of thought. It is thus crucial to understand what this procedure consists in.

Analogy

At stake for Simondon is showing that individuation is primarily an operation, and placing knowledge of the operations of individuation at the heart of a new way of thinking about being and a new method of thought. Only an analogical method turns out to be adequate to ontogenesis, however. The founding act of this method, the analogical act, is defined as a "putting into relation of two operations" in one of the supplements to *L'individu et sa genèse physico-biologique* included in the new edition of the work (261–268; *IL*, 559–566). In the *Sophist*, Plato describes the analogical act as an act of thought that consists in "transporting an operation of thought [that has been] learned and tested with a particular known structure (for instance, the one that serves to define the fisherman in the *Sophist*) onto another particular structure [that is] unknown and the object of inquiry (the structure of the Sophist in the *Sophist*)" (*IG*, 264; *IL*, 562). Plato's discussion already makes clear that the transfer of operations is not grounded in an ontological terrain common to the two domains, in a relation of identity between the sophist and the fisherman, but rather establishes an "identity of operative relations." Whatever the difference between terms (on one side the sophist, on the other the fisherman), the operations (of productive seduction/capture) are the same.

Nonetheless, because it operates in an ontogenetic perspective, Simondon's reworking of Platonic analogy demands a rigorous definition. In effect, if transfer is only a transfer to one being of the manner in which we think about another being, analogy remains an "association of ideas." And it is not unlikely that, at the time he was pursuing this inquiry into individuation, Simondon had in mind some infelicitous examples of recourse to analogy. In particular, in his view, the greatest weakness of the then emerging science of cybernetics was undoubtedly that it functionally identified living beings with automatons (see *IG*, 26; *IL*, 28). Nonetheless, less than ten years after the birth of that science, Simondon paid homage to it in *Du mode d'existence des objets techniques*, as the first attempt at a "study of the intermediary domain between the specialized sciences" (MEOT, 49). And in fact, basing its procedure on the study of automatons, cybernetics proposed an entire series of analogies between automated systems and other systems (essentially: nervous, living, and social), in order to study them from the point of view of the "controlled acts" of which they were capable as systems. Yet, reading Simondon's definition of analogy, we understand precisely why he could not but think of cybernetics in terms of an imprecise use of analogy, which from the outset exposed it to the danger of reductionism: in effect, bringing together the logical structure of functioning of systems independently of the study of their concrete individuation leads purely and simply to identifying the systems studied—living, social, and so on—with automatons, capable only of adaptive behavior.

In such a context, the development of a rigorous understanding of analogy appears as a response to a crisis, as a matter of fending off a diluted conception of analogy, which would deprive it of its richness. This is why Simondon specifies that the analogical method, which posits the autonomy of operations in relation to their terms, is valid only insofar as it sticks to an ontological postulate stipulating that structures must be known by the operations that energize them and not the inverse. It only has epistemological value if "the transfer of a logical operation is the transfer of an operation that reproduces the operative schema of the being known" (*IG*, 264–265; *IL*, 562–563).

Analogical knowledge thus establishes a relation between the operations of individuals existing outside thought and the operations of thought itself. The analogy between two beings, from the point of view of their operations, supposes an analogy between the operations of each being that is known and the operations of thought. Thus the rigorously analogical dimension of the method accounts for the parallelism mentioned previously. We may speak of a *coindividuation* of thinking and the beings thus known, whereby the method gains an immanent legitimacy: "The possibility of employing an analogical transduction to *think* a domain of reality indicates that this domain *is* effectively the seat of a transductive structuration" (*IG*, 31; *IL*, 33, emphasis mine). Here, the possibility of thinking is not capable of any excess over the real, which immediately restores the movement of being. As he pushes his inquiry into the limits of reason as far as possible, Simondon shows signs of complete confidence in the power of thought. And yet, we could not possibly be farther from the Hegelian postulate wherein only the rational is effective within being. If it began with such a postulate, analogical knowledge would not be able to grasp the "real" operations in which structures are constituted, but would stop at the apprehension of relations that are only conceptual. If we apprehend the movement of being on the basis of the identity of the rational and the real, we grasp a movement that is "only" that of spirit. Rather than pursuing the parallel operations of individuation of beings and of thought as in the theory of individuation, we will perceive only one individuation, that of Spirit, sweeping everything else along under the rubric of provisional moments. This is essentially the criticism that Simondon levels at the Hegelian dialectic: the dialectic sees only moments, whereas it is a matter of discerning phases; it makes the negative the logical motor of being; it is incapable of perceiving the richness of the preindividual tension between physical potentials that are incompatible without being opposed. Thus, where for Hegel it is on the side of thought that the identity of thinking and being is effectuated, in Simondon's philosophy such an identity rests on the transductive ground of being, which is the ground from which thought proceeds.

Nonetheless, something seems to cast doubt on the immanence of the method of thought required by the theory of individuation. It is the strange impression of dealing with analogy by "squaring."[6] In effect, analogy's power of discovery in the order of thought is itself conceived by analogy with the operation of crystallization in the domain of physical individuation: "from the microscopic crystalline seed, one can produce a monocrystal of several cubic decimeters. Doesn't the activity of thinking harbor a comparable process, mutatis mutandi?" (*IPC*, 62; *IL*, 549). In her contribution to the conference devoted to Simondon in April 1992, Anne Fagot-Largeault concludes from this passage that the "fecundity of this analogical procedure of thinking is itself explained by a physical analogy."[7] And yet, this circle of the physical and noetic is far from being a vicious one. Surely we need to recognize in it the sign of the transductive method that Simondon is putting to work, because, just as we must not look outside a domain for the structures of resolution that operate within the domain, we cannot claim to study individuation *in general*. We are always dealing only with singular *cases* of individuation, which complicates the task of a global theory of individuation. Simondon solves this difficulty by constituting a paradigm.

The Physical Paradigm

We can never place enough emphasis on the singular nature of the relation between thinking and being established by the philosophy of individuation. Thus it is not only being that must be known from the operations that energize it. Thought itself proceeds by operations that establish new relations in the order of ideas, to the point where "the primitive notional choice is invested with a self-justifying value; it is defined by the operation that constitutes it more than by the reality it objectively aims for" (*IG*, 256; *IL*, 554). As we have seen, the study of individuation requires thinking that is neither inductive nor deductive but only transductive; thought does not seek its norm anywhere else but within the field of reality initially chosen as the field of investigation. This is why the second gesture of the analogical method turns out to be *constructive*. Thought is constructed from an initial domain providing it with norms of validity and conferring upon it an evident historicity. According to Simondon, "all thought, precisely to the extent that it is real, . . . involves a historical aspect in its genesis. Real thought is *self-justifying* but not justified before being structured" (*IG*, 82; *IL*, 84). Like all *real* being, like any fragment of the real that is individuated, thought is rooted in a milieu, which constitutes its historical dimension; thoughts are not ahistorical, not stars in the heaven of ideas. They emerge from a theoretical environment, drawing the seeds of their development from it; but of course, not everything is a seed for thought, and all thought entails operative selection within the theoretical milieu of the era in which it is immersed. Taking on structure through its selective inscription in an era, thought gradually resolves its problems, and in resolving them, justifies itself.

In this way, in its faithfulness to the progression from simple to complex that characterizes the constructive method, the line of inquiry bearing on the individuation of beings will turn to the domain where this question was first posed: the physical domain, which is the "first domain in which an operation of individuation can exist" (*IG*, 231; *IL*, 319). This is why the study of the constitution of physical beings is deemed paradigmatic. But is it really the *study* of physical beings—that is, the knowledge that the physical sciences provide us—that is taken as the paradigm for the study of individuation, or is it the physical individuals themselves, their process of constitution? Simondon's formulations fluctuate between the two possibilities, now evoking crystallization (and not crystallography) as the instance of a "physical paradigm" apt to clarify the notion of metastability (*IG*, 24; *IL*, 26), while insisting elsewhere on the attempt to "draw a paradigm from the physical sciences" (*IG*, 231; *IL*, 319). Such indiscernibility between epistemological and ontological levels, evident in the formulations the author chooses to explain his choice of physical paradigm, does not stem from a lack of rigor. Rather, it ensues from choosing the process of constitution of the physical individual (and among all the physical individuals, crystals, and particles) for the paradigm of individuation, which necessarily means relying on existing descriptions of exemplary individuations. This is why the study of individuation, taking the operation constituting the physical individual for its paradigmatic operation, claims to "draw its paradigm from the physical sciences," whose criteria for validity have already been constituted "through the progress of a constructive experience" (*IG*, 257; *IL*, 555). Indeed, physics has for some time shown its "capacity for progressively transforming theory into hypotheses and then into almost directly tangible realities" (*IG*, 256; *IL*, 554), that is, a capacity for constituting the concrete from the abstract, for producing a concrete on which one may act.[8]

But what precisely will the philosophy of individuation borrow from physics? Within the initial domain constituted by physical science—and especially within the continuist and discontinuist theories that Simondon strives to prove compatible—it is a matter of pinpointing the "epistemological role" played by the notion of the individual, as well as the "phenomenological contents" to which it refers.[9] Then, on the strength of results from this initial research, it is a matter of attempting to transfer them "to domains [coming] logically and ontologically after" (*IG*, 257; *IL*, 555). They come logically after, because the constructive method proceeds from simple to complex; they come ontologically after, because the passages from physical to biological, and from physiological to psychic, correspond to successive dephasings of being. But, even though we can draw a paradigm from the physical sciences that to some extent constitutes a guiding schema for the study of individuation, this does not mean that we may claim "to operate a reduction of the vital to the physical" when transposing the physical paradigm into the domain of the living. The theory of individuation takes into account differences between the diverse levels of individuation, and "the transposition of the schema is in turn accompanied by a composition of it" (*IG*, 231; *IL*, 319). Under these conditions, by means

of this transfer from one domain to another, the philosophy of individuation itself is constructed, because it allows us to "pass from physical individuation to organic individuation, from organic individuation to psychic
individuation, and from psychic individuation to subjective and objective
transindividual, which defines the layout of this research" (*IG*, 31; *IL*, 33).
We pass from one domain of being to another by the transfer of operations
from one structure to another, while adding to each level the specificities
that the physical paradigm, because too simple, does not allow us to grasp.
*Nonetheless, the physical paradigm remains in its capacity as elementary para-
digm*; and, as Gilbert Hottois aptly stresses,[10] the original analogy of the
physical individuation of the crystal persists throughout the description of
collective individuation, wherein Simondon defines the group as a "syn-
crystallization of many individual beings" (*IPC*, 183; *IL*, 298).

The Allagmatic

"Allagmatic" is the title of the final supplemental section of *L'individu et
sa genèse physico-biologique* (IG, 261–268; *IL*, 559–566), added at the time of
its republication. Operation, transduction, analogy, and constructivism are
among the notions subsumed under this enigmatic term. The allagmatic is
first defined as "the theory of operations" (*IG*, 261; *IL*, 559), complemen-
tary to the theory of structures elaborated in the sciences. In other words,
it would appear to be a matter of the "operational side of scientific theory"
(*IG*, 263; *IL*, 561). But what is an operation? Simondon's answer is clear:
"An operation is conversion of a structure into another structure" (ibid.). It
follows, then, that we cannot define an operation *outside* a structure; and
so, defining the operation "comes back to defining a certain convertibility
of operation into structure and of structure into operation" (ibid.). One
might symbolize this relation between operation and structure, constitutive
of the notion of operation, much as Marx symbolizes the nature of the capitalist relation between commodity and money in exchange.[11] The process
through which one sells a commodity to buy another can be written in the
form: C-M-C (where C stands for *commodity*, and M for *money*). It consists
of two opposed acts: sale (C-M) and purchase (M-C), two half-chains of a
single act, since "the transformation of the commodity into money is at the
same time a transformation of money into commodity."[12] But Marx shows
that the form C-M-C (selling to buy) has as its corollary the form M-C-M
(buying to sell), which is fundamentally different because it describes the
becoming-capital of money. In this second form, in effect, commodity and
money "function only as different modes of existence of value itself."[13] The

transformation of the form C-M-C into the form M-C-M thus expresses the passage from traditional exchange to capitalist exchange, in which money and commodity are two faces of capital that enter into the process of value.

In any case, for the moment, let us look at the first definition, cited above, that Simondon proposes for the operation (O) as conversion of a structure (S) into another structure: that definition can be written in the form S-O-S, entailing a contraction of the half-chain S-O (conversion of a first structure into operation) and of the half-chain O-S (conversion of the operation into the next structure). Such a formulation shows that the allagmatic is concerned with modulation, that is, with the putting into relation of an operation and a structure. Yet, a few lines later, Simondon proposes the second definition already cited, in which the operation entails convertibility of the operation into structure and the structure into operation; we now see that this second definition constitutes a variation on the first, and may be written in the form O-S-O, wherein the focus is now on the passage from one operation to another by way of a structure.

It now becomes possible to define the allagmatic more precisely than Simondon's initial definition of it as a theory of operations. At the levels of being and thought, the allagmatic involves a double becoming, ontological (or rather ontogenetic) and epistemological: on the one hand, it is a matter of the allagmatic "determining the true relation between structure and operation within *being*"; but, on the other hand, it falls to the allagmatic "to organize the rigorous and valid relation between structural knowledge and operative knowledge of a being, between *analytical science* and *analogical science*" (*IG*, 267; *IL*, 565). Evidently, the nuance of the term allagmatic cannot be confined to a simple affirmation of the analogical dimension of knowledge, which consists in knowing a structure through its operations. Yet, to the extent that the allagmatic invites us to ask "what is the relation between operation and structure within being?" (*IG*, 266; *IL*, 564), it becomes clear that we cannot rely entirely on analytical science, which assumes that a whole is reducible to the sum of its parts, or on analogical science, which assumes a functional holism in which the whole is primordial and expressed through its operation. Allagmatic theory is concerned with grasping the union, within being, of the structure of a being and its holist functioning; this is why it can be defined as *"the study of individual being"* (*IG*, 267; *IL*, 565). Apprehended from the point of view of the individuating process whence it emerges, the individual is not a definitive being, finished upon arrival. It is the partial and provisional result of individuation in that it harbors a preindividual reserve within itself that makes it susceptible to plural individuations.

Grasping being "prior to any distinction or opposition between operation and structure," the allagmatic entails constructing a point of view that comprises the individual as "that in which an operation can be reconverted into structure, and a structure into operation." This is another way of saying that the allagmatic is concerned with changes of state, or once again, relation. But we must immediately add that relation would no longer be conceived of as something that "springs up between two terms that are already individuated": in effect, within the theory of individuation, relation is redefined as "an aspect of the internal resonance of a system of individuation" (*IG*, 27; *IL*, 29). In this respect, it has a "rank of being" and cannot be considered as an entirely logical reality.

The Reality of the Relative

From Knowing the Relation to Knowing as Relation

"The method consists in trying not to piece together the essence of a reality by means of a conceptual relation between two final terms, and in considering any true relation as having a rank of being" (*IG*, 30; *IL*, 32). It is in such terms, precisely on the basis of a methodological concern, that Simondon chooses to present the postulate of the reality of relation, but only insofar as this postulate *sums up* the method on its own ("The method consists in . . ."). Insofar as this simple statement of method is simultaneously an ontological statement, a thesis on being—as is always the case with Simondon, as we have rather insistently noted—it can be read as a declaration of war against the substantialist tradition, to which we owe the persistent misunderstanding of relation, conceived as a simple relation between terms that preexist the act of putting them into relation. "It is because terms are conceived as substances that relation is a relationship between terms, and being is separated into terms because it is conceived as substance, primitively, prior to any examination of individuation" (ibid.). Inverting this traditional point of view, the study of individuation makes substance into "an extreme instance of relation, that of the inconsistency of relation" (*IG*, 233; *IL*, 321). A substance appears when a term absorbs into itself the relation that gave rise to it, thus obscuring it. As long as being is understood substantially, relation appears as nothing but a mental connection between a substance and attributes or qualities conceivable outside it. The substantialist approach is thus incapable of apprehending a being, for instance, a sulfur crystal, other than by conceptually adding predicates, such as the color yellow, opacity, transparency, and so on, to the idea of crystalline matter. Yet Simondon shows that the characteristics of individuation that appear when we study the formation of crystalline forms of a same type (here: sulfur) are not "qualities" insofar as "such characteristics are prior to any idea of substance (since we are dealing with the same body)" (*IG*, 75; *IL*, 77). Transparency and opacity in particular can characterize the same form (sulfur crystal) in succession as a function of the temperature imposed on the metastable system at the moment of crystallization. Transparency and opacity thus cannot be thought of as qualities of a substance, but as characteristics appearing in a system undergoing a change of state.[14] We must cease to apprehend being as a substance or a compound of substances if we are to cease understanding relation as that which links, within thought, elements separated within being. This is why only a theory that thinks being through the multiplicity of operations whereby it is individuated is equal to transforming our approach to relation, such that we may understand it as "relation in being, relation of being, manner of being" (*IG*, 30; *IL*, 32). Being itself now appears as that which becomes *by linking together*.

Recall that, when Simondon posits the realism of relation as a "postulate of inquiry" (*IG*, 82; *IL*, 84) in *L'individu et sa genèse physico-biologique*, it is in the context of a passage in which the stakes are methodological, since it is a matter of defining knowledge. Yet it soon becomes apparent that knowledge cannot be conceived as a simple relationship between these two substances (that is, the knowing subject and the object known); rather we must conceive of it as a "*relation of two relations* of which the one is in the domain of the object and the other in the domain of the subject" (*IG*, 81; *IL*, 83). If it is true, in fact, that relation is not something that links together two preexisting terms[15] but is something that arises by constituting the terms themselves *as* relations, then we understand how knowledge can appear as a relation of relations. The parallelism between the operation of knowing and the operation known may be explained in the final instance as a modality of relation; this explanation allows us to correct the idea of separate, autonomous realities that the term parallelism might suggest: the distinct operations that constitute the *knowing* subject and the *known* object are in effect unified in the act of a relation that is called *knowledge*. But why does Simondon insist on specifying, in a phrase in which the use of italics makes it appear as decisive as it feels redundant: "*The epistemological postulate of this study is that relation between two relations is itself a relation*" (ibid.)? That relation between two relations is itself a relation is precisely what seems obvious. We can only understand the author's insistence on this point if we envision the ontological implications of the formulation; then we see that knowledge, insofar as it is a "relation between two relations," "is itself a relation," which is to say, knowledge *exists in the same mode as the beings that it links together, considered from the point of view of that which constitutes their reality.* Put otherwise, it follows from the postulate of the reality of relation that what makes for the reality of knowledge, and of all being for that matter, is *being a relation.*

Consistency and Constitution

Simondon's examination of the individuation of physical beings leads him to draw on references from the experimental sciences; yet it quickly becomes apparent that his step in this direction, toward the experimental sciences, is motivated by the fact that the knowledge they provide is knowledge of relation and thus "can only provide philosophical analysis with a being consisting in relations" (*IG*, 82; *IL*, 84). There are two ways of understanding the fact that the individual consists in relations: on the one hand, a physical individual is nothing other than the relation or relations (a single individuating operation or reiterated individuations) that have given birth to it by making it a bridge between disparate orders of being; on the other hand, in keeping with the second meaning of the verb *to consist*, we gather that relation gives consistency to being, and any physical individual acquires its consistency, that is, its reality, from its relational activity.

Thus we may put a new twist on Hegel's famous words in the preface to *Principles of the Philosophy of the Right*, according to which "What is rational is real, and what is real is rational."[16] With its articulation of reversibility, Hegel's formulation constructs an identity between the effectivity of the real (the German term used here is *wirklich*) and the movement of effectuation of Spirit. In contrast, we might say: "What is relational is real, and what is real is relational." In our formulation, as in Hegel's, reversibility does not prevent deeper gradation. In effect, what Hegel aims to make clear is not only that the rational is real (which amounts to saying that reason is not defined by its exclusion from the sphere of the effective), but also, and more importantly, that the real, properly understood, identifies with the rational (put otherwise, only what occurs as a movement of reason is effective). In an analogous manner, we might say not only that relation is real, but even more, that it is relation that constitutes being, that is, what is real in beings. And the postulate of the realism of relation seems to imply a gradation, to wit: as soon as we recognize its value as being, we discover that relation is what makes for the being of the individual, whereby an individual comes to be as such. This is made clear in the passages describing the individuation of physical beings, such as this one: "When we say that, for the physical individual, relation is of being, we do not mean that relation *expresses* being [e.g., the physical individual] but that it constitutes it" (*IG*, 126; *IL*, 128).

If we are to treat this subversion of the Hegelian formula as something more than a play on words in which the movement of reason as the motor of becoming gives way to the constituting activity of relation, we must avoid extracting a general statement from it (of the type: "Being is relation"), for this would undermine the central postulate wherein a theory of individuation always and necessarily proceeds from cases. We are studying not individuation in general, but individuation of a physical being *or* a living being, of a crystal *or* an electron, of a plant *or* an animal, and the characteristics of individuation of the living being become apparent only upon the specific study of a specific group of living beings (coelenterates, for instance) insofar as it brings out the differences with individuation of physical beings. We may say, then, that relation constitutes the being of the physical individual, of the living being, of the psychic subject, and so on, in a manner that is in each instance singular. There exists, however, a certain number of characteristics common to operations of individuation as a whole, without which there would be no sense in attempting a study of individuation of the sort Simondon undertakes. In particular, an operation of individuation only occurs within a system harboring enough potential energy for the onset of a singularity (that is, a structuring seed) to activate a taking on of form. The taking on of form always operates as a putting into relation of two orders of magnitude between which there has been no previous communication. Thus, to return to an example already discussed, a plant is defined by instituting a relation between the cosmic order of light and the inframolecular order of minerals, to the point where it might be defined as an "interelemental node" (*IG*, 32–33, note 12; *IL*, 34–35, note 12) that *through itself* brings into communication the minerals contained in the Earth and the luminous energy emitted by the Sun. Ultimately, we can best understand the postulate of the realism of relation through the relational activity that defines the individual genetically: relation is real insofar as the individual is relational; but reciprocally, the individual obtains its reality from the relation constituting it; which might be stated in a general formulation: "The individual is the reality of a constituting relation, not the interiority of a constituted term" (*IG*, 60; *IL*, 62). The individual may be understood as the "activity of relation"—it is at once what acts in the relation and what results from it; the individual is what is constituted in relation, or more precisely, *as* relation: it is the transductive reality of relation; "it is the being *of* relation" (*IG*, 61; *IL*, 63).

Already at the level of physical beings, that relation is constituting means that interiority and exteriority are not substantially different; there are not two domains, but a relative distinction; because, insofar as any individual is capable of growth, what was exterior to it can become interior. We may say then that relation, insofar as it is constituting, exists as a limit. As a function of this constituting power of the limit, the individual appears not as a finite being but as a limited being, that is, as a being in which "the dynamism of growth never stops" (*IG*, 91; *IL*, 93). What characterizes individuals is not finitude. Finitude for Simondon connotes an incapacity for growth, signaling a lack of preindividual being that is required for amplification in existence. Rather, what characterizes the individual is limitation, which comes of the capacity of the limit to be displaced. The individual is not finished but limited, that is, capable of indefinite growth. The individuation of a crystal offers undoubtedly the purest example of this constituting power of relation as limit; provided that we respect the required conditions, we need only put a crystal back in its solution to see it grow in all directions. During growth, the limit of the crystal plays the role of a structural seed, which is displaced as the crystal grows larger. Simondon explains the capacity of the crystal for growth in terms of its periodic structure (a periodicity comparable to the repetition of the motif of a tapestry). Because of its periodic structure, the crystal has no center, and its limit "is virtually at all points" (*IG*, 93; *IL*, 95) and is thus not an envelope for any interiority. For Simondon, following the theory of relativity, the electron, as a physical individual, is much the same. Like the crystal, the particle "is not *concentric until a limit of interiority constituting the substantial domain of the individual*, but on the very limit of being" (*IG*, 125; *IL*, 127). Where the atomists of antiquity defined the atom as a substantial being determined by dimension, mass, and fixed form, in other words, as a being capable of remaining identical to itself through change, the theory of relativity makes the definition of a particle depend on its relation to other particles. If it is true that the mass of a particle varies as a function of its speed, then any sort of random encounter modifying the speed of a particle is enough to modify its mass. We may say then that "any modification of the relation of a particle to others is also a modification of its internal characteristics" (ibid.), and thus the individual consistency of a particle is entirely relative.

This Relation That Is the Individual

As is probably already clear, "relative" is by no means synonymous with "unreal." This is why Simondon can only oppose the probabilistic theory of the individual defended by Niels Bohr, among others, according to which "the appearance of the physical individual is relative to the measuring subject" (*IG*, 140; *IL*, 142). In this case, the being-relative of the individual implies its nonreality, because relation itself, defined as an artifact of human measurement, is devoid of reality: "at the limit, relation is nothing, it is only the probability for relation between terms [that is, measuring subject and measured physical individual] to be established here or there" (*IG*, 141; *IL*, 143). Defined in probabilistic terms by the existence of a formal relation, the individual would have nothing real about it. To define the physical individual as a being relative to a subject measuring it is to make it an inconsistent being. It is only when the individual exists as the operator of a relation within a system of the same order of magnitude that its relativity ceases to be the mark of its unreality. But then it is no longer understood as relative to human measurement, but as relative to an *associated milieu* that is born as its complement at the same time, which is the form in which the preindividual subsists after the operation of individuation. In the case of the individuation of the crystal, the associated milieu is the solution in which the potential energy of the system resides. In the domain of physical individuation, Simondon rethinks the associated milieu as *field*. As its "true physical magnitude" (*IG*, 132; *IL*, 134), the field is "centered around" the individual without being a part of it. Not to be confused with a simple probability of appearance, the field expresses the property that a physical particle possesses of being polarized, that is, of being defined by the interaction that it has with other physical particles. Unless we grasp the importance of its relation with an associated milieu, we do not understand what the reality of the individual consists in: the individual, in effect, is not an absolute; by itself alone, it is an incomplete reality, incapable of expressing the entirety of being; and yet it is not illusory either, and, associated with a milieu of the same order of magnitude retaining the preindividual, the individual acquires the consistency of a relation. The significance of the previous discussion of the allagmatic in terms of the construction of a point of view capable of grasping the individual as "that in which an operation can be reconverted into structure and a structure into operation" is now much clearer: the individual alone is not capable of such a reconversion, but, insofar as it is inseparable from its associated milieu, it is capable. Thus the allagmatic shows how the individual is neither absolute nor illusory but relative; it has the reality of a relational act.

Without a doubt, the ontological postulate, or rather, the ontogenetic postulate, central to a philosophy of individuation is that individuals *consist* in relations, and as a consequence, relation has the status of being and constitutes being. Indeed we can only approach Simondon's specific theses on psychosocial reality on the basis of this postulate. Nonetheless, if, above and beyond differences of domain, this postulate illuminates the real center in beings that is common to them and that renders them conjointly comprehensible, does it not prevent us from taking into account the difference between domains? And if there is not a substantial difference between individuals belonging to different domains of being, for example between physical individuals and living beings, if the difference that holds them apart is not that which separates two genera, how to arrive at a definition of distinct *domains*?

Such a question does not present a crisis for the philosophy of individuation but serves to clarify the specificity of its procedures. The difference separating two domains such as the physical and the living is not one of substance, and these two domains are not opposed as "living matter and nonliving matter." Rather, the difference between them is that which distinguishes "a primary individuation in inert systems and a secondary individuation in living systems" (*IG*, 149; *IL*, 151). What differentiates two domains, then, lies in the individuation giving birth to the individuals populating each domain. What does this mean? It means that we must conceive of biological individuation not as something that adds determinations to an already physically individuated being, but as a slowing down of physical individuation, as a bifurcation that operates prior to the physical level proper. It is by diving back into the level of the preindividual prior to physical individuation that the individuation of a living being begins: "Phenomena of a lower order of magnitude, which we call microphysical, are not in fact physical or vital, but prephysical and prevital; the purely physical, not alive, would only begin at a supermolecular scale; it is at this level that individuation brings forth the crystal or the mass of protoplasmic matter" (*IG*, 149–150; *IL*, 151–152). But this bifurcation does not give birth to genera of being in the form of inert matter and life, for instance, genera that we might then mysteriously subdivide into species, with the plant and animal then appearing as specific subdivisions of the living. The difference between plants and animals is explained in a manner similar to the difference between the physical and the vital. Thus the animal appears to the observer of individuation as "an inchoate plant" (*IG*, 150; *IL*, 152), that is, as a plant that was dilated at the very beginning of its becoming; more precisely, animal individuation "finds sustenance at the most primitive phase of plant individuation, retaining something prior to the development into an adult plant, and in particular the capacity of receiving information over a long period of time" (ibid.). Between the physical and the vital, between the plant and the animal, we need look not for substantial differences that lend themselves to founding distinctions between genus and species, but rather for differences in speed in the process of their formation. What divides being into domains is ultimately nothing other than *the rhythm of becoming*, sometimes speeding through stages, sometimes slowing to resume individuation at the very beginning.

Such observations about the heterogeneity of individuating rhythms make it possible to speak about what constitutes the difference between "physical beings" and "living beings." Living individuals differ from physical individuals in that they add a second "perpetual individuation that is life itself" to the first instantaneous individuation wherein they arise as complements of a milieu (*IG*, 25; *IL*, 27). As such, a living being is not only a result but also, and more profoundly, a "theater of individuation" (ibid.). In contrast to a crystal or electron, a living being is not content to be individuated to its limit, that is, to grow along its outer edge: "The living individual has . . . true interiority, because individuation takes place within it; the interior is constituting in the living individual, while only the limit is constituting in the physical individual, and what is topologically interior is genetically anterior. The living individual is contemporary to itself in all its elements, while the physical individual is not, comprising a past that is radically past, even when it is still in the process of growing" (*IG*, 26; *IL*, 28). The physical individual does not comprise a true interiority, since its interiority is of the past insofar as it entails a process of sedimentation, whereas the living being does not cease individuating within itself, which is why it exists in the present. In addition to an exterior milieu, living beings possess an interior milieu, such that their existence appears as a perpetual putting into relation of the interior milieu and the exterior milieu, which relation the individual operates within itself. The living individual is capable both of relations oriented toward its interior (regeneration, as internal genesis, being a prime example) and of relations exerted toward the exterior, such as reproduction.

At this level, however, we need to distinguish between living beings. There are those considered "superior" because they are endowed with autonomy. And there are those of the colony type, where it is not entirely clear if the true individual is the entire colony as a functioning totality or its elements; insofar as these elements remain content to carry out specialized functions, they behave in effect more as organs than as individuals. Simondon resolves this problem by looking at the passage from being-organ to being-individual with reference to the function of reproduction. What individualizes an individual living in a colony, in relationship to the colony in which it lives, is the moment when it detaches from the colony in order to lay an egg that gives rise to an individual-strain, which may form a new colony by budding. In sum, what confers separate individuality on a living being is its thanatological character[17]—the fact of detaching from the original colony and, after having reproduced, dying at a distance from it. Although the example of coelenterates on which Simondon bases his description of the individuation of living beings may appear surprising, or even poorly chosen in light of the difficulty in this case of precisely determining the site of individuality, it does not seem to me that the author made this choice lightly. This example provides an observatory for studying the very *constitution* of individuality as a relational activity. The individual here is pure relation: it exists *between* two colonies, without being integrated into either, and its activity is an activity of amplification of being.

More generally, attention to the specificity of the mode of existence of biological individuals affords new insights into the notion of relation as Simondon understands it. In effect, if we choose to describe the interior relation of the individual to itself as a relation between the individual and "subindividuals" that may enter into its composition, and if we do not forget that the living individual is also in a constituting relation to the group to which it belongs, that is, to a sort of natural community (society of ants, bees, etc.), we see that "The relation between the singular being and the group is the same as between the individual and subindividuals. In this sense, it is possible to say that, between the different hierarchic scales of the same individual and between the group and the individual, there exists a homogeneity of relation" (*IG*, 158; *IL*, 160). There is no difference in nature between the relation of the individual to the group and its relation to itself; such is the lesson that is finally drawn from the postulate of the reality of relation. A single relation runs through all levels of being, because ultimately, what unifies being in itself, unifying each being, is the activity of relation.

The Transindividual Relation

Psychic and Collective Individuation: One or Many Individuations?

Among the unusual features of Simondon's work, not least is his thinking on the nature of the relation established between individual and collective in the context of human societies through the study of psychic and collective individuation, which process he describes in minute detail in *L'individuation psychique et collective*, the eponymous work following *L'individu et sa genèse psycho-biologique*. To indicate what the book is about, he chooses a title that is as striking as it is enigmatic: he refers us neither to the "individuation of the collective" nor to "psychic and collective individuations," but rather "psychic and collective individuation"; in other words, one individuation bringing together two terms across the unifying distance of an "and."

The use of the singular in the title makes clear that the work will address a single individuation, psychic *and* collective, or to put it another way, *psychosocial*, as Simondon sometimes writes, suppressing in a single stroke the problematic status of the "and." The book, then, is about an individuation with two faces, a single operation with two products or results: psychic being and the collective.

Nonetheless, in the introduction, he specifies that it is a matter of "two individuations . . . in reciprocal relationship to one another" (*IPC*, 19; *IL*, 29). But "reciprocal" does not mean "identical": a relation is said to be reciprocal when it is simultaneously exerted from the first term to the second, and inversely. To say that psychic individuation and collective individuation are reciprocal to some extent amounts to making them into poles of a single constituting relation. First and foremost, however, to say they are reciprocal is to say that two individuations are involved, of which the first (psychic individuation) is said to be "interior" to the individual, and the second "exterior."

In the passage already cited, in the context of the reciprocity of the two individuations, the concept of transindividual is introduced: "the two individuations, psychic and collective . . . allow us to define a category of transindividual that tries to take into account their systematic unity" (*IPC*, 19; *IL*, 29). What might such a unity consist of? Insofar as the two individuations are initially designated—at the beginning of the same paragraph—as "the relation interior and exterior to the individual," the transindividual appears not as that which unifies individual and society, but as a relation interior to the individual (defining its psyche) and a relation exterior to the individual (defining the collective): the transindividual unity of two relations is thus a relation of relations.

Psychic and collective individuation would thus be the unity of two reciprocal individuations, psychic individuation and collective individuation. It seems, however, that we cannot rest with this response. In fact, as soon as we look a bit closer at the study of psychic individuation, we find it to be compound: emotion and perception thus appear as "two psychic individuations prolonging the individuation of the living being" (*IPC*, 120; *IL*, 260). If psychic individuation is compound, we are no longer faced with two individuations (psychic and collective) but with a multiplicity of individuations. But then, how many individuations are there, exactly, and how can these multiple individuations be finally unified in a single *psychic and collective individuation*?

None of this makes sense unless we remember that the entire project of a philosophy of individuation is guided by an antisubstantialist ambition, which amounts to saying: psyche is not a substance. In effect, the aim is to arrive at thinking psyche and the collective "without calling on new substances" (*IPC*, 19; *IL*, 29), such as "soul" or "society," which would be new substances in relationship to those already at our disposal at the end of the study pursued in *L'individu et sa genèse physico-biologique*, namely: psychic individual and living being. Clearly, then, the project runs two risks, which are stated at the outset: "psychologism" and "sociologism," two substantialisms that await any thinking about the reality designated as "psychosocial," ready to pin that reality onto fixed entities (psyche and society).

But what does it mean to think the reality of psychic being and the collective without calling on new substances? It means showing that psychic individuation and collective individuation *prolong* vital individuation, that they are the continuation of it. As individuated beings, living beings spring from a first, biological individuation. But, as we have already begun to see, living beings only maintain their existence by perpetuating this first individuation from which they emerged through a series of *individualizing* individuations. This continuation of the first individuation is called *individualization*. In effect, a living being, "in order to exist, needs to be able to continue individualizing by resolving problems in the milieu surrounding it, which is its milieu" (*IPC*, 126; *IL*, 264). In the analysis proposed by Simondon, perception, for instance, appears as an act of individuation operated by a living being to resolve a conflict into which it has entered with its milieu. In his view, to perceive is not primarily to grasp a form; rather it is the act taking place within an ensemble constituted by the relation between subject and world, through which a subject invents a form and thereby modifies its own structure and that of the object at the same time: we see only within a system in tension, of which we are a subensemble. Taking the example of the astonishing aptitude of children for recognizing different body parts of animals when seeing them for the first time, including ones whose morphology is very different from that of humans, Simondon concludes that the child is bodily engaged in perception as a function of the emotion—sympathy, fear, and so on—provoked by the animal. As such, it is never merely the form of the animal that is perceived but "its orientation as a whole, its polarity that indicates whether it is lying down or standing up, whether it is facing or fleeing, taking a hostile or trustworthy stance" (*IPC*, 79; *IL*, 236). If we admit that psychic individuation consists of a series of individuations that prolong the first individuation of the living being, we will then conclude: "Each thought, each conceptual discovery, each surge of affection reprises the first individuation; thought develops as a reprise of this schema of the first individuation, of which it is a distant rebirth, partial but faithful" (*IPC*, 127; *IL*, 264).

As we know, the first individuation is that of giving birth to the individuated living being. But what is born of psychic individuation? A new type of individual, the psychic individual? Apparently not. Simondon's introduction already informed us that "psyche is made of successive individuations allowing for the being to resolve problematic states corresponding to the permanent putting into communication of what is larger than it with what is smaller than it" (*IPC*, 22; *IL*, 31), thus making clear that it is more a question of psychic *problems* than a psychic individual. Only two sorts of individuals exist: physical individuals and living individuals. This is why, if we are to be rigorous, we must say that there "*is not properly speaking a psychic individuation*, but an individualization of the living being giving birth to the somatic and the psychic" (*IPC*, 134; *IL*, 268; emphasis added). Psychic individuation is a perpetuation of vital individuation.

What we loosely call *psychic individuation* thus appears as the operation that, *in an already individuated being*, carries on with an initial individuation;

consequently, it can give birth not to a new individual but rather to a new domain of being. From the outset, in effect, the definition given by Simondon of the individual as "reality of a metastable relation" (*IPC*, 79–80; *IL*, 237) invalidates an approach based on preconstituted domains; such domains are dependent on the modality of individuation, and do not pre-exist it. Domains are a result of the manner in which the metastability of the individual/milieu system is conserved or, on the contrary, degraded after individuation. The physical domain, then, is that wherein the individual, in appearing, causes the metastable state to disappear, by suppressing the tensions within the system in which it appears; in contrast, the domain of the living being is defined by the fact that the individual maintains the metastability of the system in which it arose. But to return to the "psychic domain" supposedly born from psychic individuation, what will permit us to define it, given that there exist no psychic individuals in the sense in which there exist physical and living individuals? Posing the question in this way is not entirely correct, since it implies that domains of being may be defined by the types of individuals populating them. Yet, insofar as domains depend on the modality of individuation, and insofar as the modality conserves or does not conserve the metastability of the system, domains are not defined by the types of individuals that fill them, for these also result from the individuating operation. Nonetheless, even after such qualifications, the question remains: What allows us to define a domain of being?

In light of this question, let's return to the previously cited assertion by Simondon that there "is not properly speaking a psychic individuation but an individualization of the living being that gives birth to the somatic and psychic." To understand this, we need to recall that, as long as it lives, a living being never ceases to run into a series of problems: perception, nourishment, feeling an emotion, for instance, appear as so many attempts to resolve this or that problem of compatibility with the milieu. Furthermore, such compatibilization of the organism with the milieu may take the form of a doubling of the vital psychosomatic unity in accordance with two series of functions: vital or somatic functions and psychic functions. Psychic individuation then appears as a new structuration of the living being, which is distributed into *two distinct domains*: the somatic domain and the psychic domain. Where there was previously a homogeneous psychosomatic unity, there is, after individuation, a "functional and relational" unity. And so, we reach the point where we can answer the question posed above: what defines a domain of being are not the *substances* filling it, but the *functions* born of the individuating doubling, which give it its name.

If we stay with this description of psychosomatic duality as the result of a doubling operation within the living being and not as dualism of substances, it becomes possible for us to reconsider the separation of human and animal. The traditional opposition between human and animal depends, in effect, on a substantialist dualism of somatic and psychic, whereby the animal is confined to somatic behaviors: "In contrast with the human who perceives, the animal appears perpetually to feel without being able to raise itself to the level of representing the object separate from its contact with the object" (*IPC*, 140; *IL*, 271–272). Still, animals have behaviors of individualization, even if these are less numerous than the instinctual behaviors arising from individuation; such behaviors of individualization are behaviors of "organized reaction," which imply the invention of a structure on the part of the living being. Consequently, the difference between human and animal appears as one "of level rather than of nature" (*IPC*, 141; *IL*, 272); and the implications of this anthropological antiessentialism for thinking the collective are numerous.

An attentive examination of psychic individuation discovers more individualization than individuation, and elsewhere Simondon presents such individualization as "interior individuation" (*IPC*, 19; *IL*, 29). Still, it might seem odd to qualify as "interior" an individuation that, through perception and action, sets up the relation to the world and to other living beings, that is, to an exteriority.

We should first consider interior individuation in opposition to so-called exterior individuation that gives birth to the collective as a reality existing outside the individual. But then we need especially to think of it in terms of the structural engagement of the individual in the psychic acts it accomplishes. Perception, for instance, is not accomplished outside the subject; perception is not seized by an exterior form; rather, perception engages the perceiving subject as part of an oriented system. The example of the child perceiving an animal already shows clearly: to perceive is to invent a form with the goal of resolving a problem of incompatibility between the perceiving subject and the world in which it exists. We may even go so far as to say that a subject only perceives or acts *outside* itself to the extent that it simultaneously operates an individuation within itself. Put another way, a subject "operates the segregation of unities in the object world of perception, which is the support for action or guarantor for sensible qualities, insofar as this subject operates in itself an individualization proceeding by successive leaps" (*IPC*, 97; *IL*, 247). For Simondon, then, as we have seen, psyche comes down to a progressive individualization within the individual. And this is precisely why psyche must not be understood as a substance. That it is said to be an "interior relation" does not then mean that it is interiority.

Neither an enclosed interior nor a pure exteriority without consistency, psyche is constituted at the intersection of a double polarity, *between* the relation to the world and others and the relation to self (without us really understanding what this now desubstantialized "self" consists in). The reality of psyche is transductive, that of a relation connecting two liaisons. This relation, as we have seen, operates in the individual as individualization; and it is operated through affectivity and emotivity, which define the "relational layer constituting the center of individuality" (*IPC*, 99; *IL*, 248). By situating the center of individuality in affectivity and emotivity, Simondon distances himself from the majority of conceptualizations of psychic individuality, which rely on a theory of consciousness or on the hypothesis of the unconscious. The true center of individuality, nonlocalized, is on the order of a subconscious: according to Simondon, the unconscious designates a too substantial reality conceived on the model of consciousness—like a reversal of it, and so Simondon will look elsewhere for what assures the liaison between relation to self and relation to the world; his inquiry brings to light the affectivo-emotive layer, the domain of intensities, which alone allows for an understanding of the global psychic reconfigurations that operate within individuals by crossing thresholds.

On this point, the author of *L'individuation psychique et collective* is quite close to the Spinozan understanding of the subject of ethics as a site of perpetual variation in its power to act, which is a function of its capacity to affect other subjects (i.e., to be the cause in them of affects that increase or diminish their power of action) and to be affected by them (i.e., to undergo the effects of their actions in the form of affects that increase or diminish the subject's own power). To the extent that the ethical difference between what is liberating and what is enslaving comes back to the difference between affects that increase our power of action and those that diminish it, we may say that the capacity to affect and be affected constitutes the center of the Spinozan theory of the subject. In Spinoza's view, consciousness, far from being a stable and autonomous entity capable of harboring free will, varies as a function of the globality of the "affective life" of the subject, that is to say, as a function of the relation of forces arising between active and passive affects within the subject, as well as within passive affects, and between joyful passions (increasing our power) and mournful passions (diminishing it). Simondon's explanation of the affectivo-emotive layer, namely, that "Modifications to it are modifications of the individual" (*IPC*, 99; *IL*, 248), is already true of the capacity to affect and to be affected in

Spinoza. And salient in such a phrasing is an understanding of the subject wherein relation to the outside is not something coming to an already constituted subject from without, but something without which the subject would not be able to be constituted.

Affectivity and Emotivity: More-Than-Individual Life

Taking up the question of psyche by problematizing psychic and collective individuation allows Simondon to break with the substantialist opposition between individual and collectivity wherein psychic life has traditionally been defined in terms of the interior life *of the individual*. In effect, Simondon opens a perspective in which "psychic reality is not closed upon itself. The psychic problematic cannot be resolved in intraindividual terms." And this is because a "psychic life wanting to be intraindividual would never be able to overcome a fundamental disparation[1] between the perceptive problematic and the affective problematic" (*IG*, 164–165; *IL*, 167).

The "perceptive problematic" is that of the existence of a multiplicity of perceptual worlds wherein it is always a matter of inventing a form inaugurating a compatibility between the milieu in which perception operates and the being that perceives; and this problematic concerns the individual as such. Why insist here that we are speaking of the individual *as such*? This is because the affective problematic is, inversely, the experience wherein a being will feel that it is not only individual. To put it more precisely, affectivity, the relational layer constituting the center of individuality, arises in us as a liaison between the relation of the individual to itself and its relation to the world. As such, it is primarily in the form of a tension that this relation to self is effectuated: *affectivity, in effect, puts the individual in relation with something that it brings with it, but that it feels quite justifiably as exterior to itself as individual.* Affectivity includes a relation between the individuated being and a share of not-yet-individuated preindividual reality that any individual carries with it: affective life, as "relation to self," is thus a relation to what, *in the self*, is not of the order of the individual.[2] Affective life thus shows us that we are not only individuals, that our being is not reducible to our individuated being.

In the language of Simondon, let us say that *the subject is the reality constituted by the individual and by the preindividual share accompanying it throughout its life*. And if the problem of the individual as such is that of perceptual worlds, "the problem of the subject is that of the heterogeneity between perceptual worlds and the affective world, *between the individual and the preindividual*" (*IPC*, 108; *IL*, 253; emphasis added). Such heterogeneity is proper to the subject as such, to the subject as subject, that is, as more-than-individual being: for "the subject is individual and more-than-individual; it is incompatible with itself" (ibid.). As we will see, this means for Simondon that the subject can truly resolve the tension characterizing it only within the collective; the subject is a being tensed toward the collective, and its reality is that of a "transitory way."

Nonetheless, the subject can be tempted—or, it would surely be more precise to say, *constrained*—to resolve this tension in an intrasubjective way. Such an attempt is destined to fail, yet according to Simondon it constitutes an experience deserving description in its own right: the experience of anxiety.

For the author of *L'individuation psychique et collective*, the description of the lived experience of anxiety plays a central role, following directly on the heels of his initial account of the notion of the transindividual in the first part entitled "Psychic Individuation." In fact, if affectivity is what makes the subject confront a share of preindividual within it which exceeds its capacity for individual absorption, such an excess can take the form of an unbearable invasion within the subject experiencing it. In Simondon's view, anxiety is thus not a passive experience; it is the effort made by a subject to resolve the experience of tension between preindividual and individuated within itself; an attempt to individuate all of the preindividual at once, as if to live it fully.

In anxiety, "the subject feels its existence as a problem posed to itself, feeling itself divided into preindividual nature and individuated being" (*IPC*, 111; *IL*, 255). This is why we may say that this experience goes "toward an end that is the polar opposite of the movement whereby one takes refuge in individuality" (ibid.); the movement of anxiety falls back on misunderstanding the presence in itself of a share of preindividual nature exceeding the constituted individual; the anxious person, far from misunderstanding this share in itself larger than the "self," makes of it a painful experience, experiencing it as a nature that cannot ever coincide with its individuated being. But the subject seeks nonetheless to remake *in itself* the unity of preindividual and individuated. To some extent, then, the experience of anxiety appears as an experimentation with something unlivable, wherein the subject makes an effort to actualize within it what, by definition, is not in keeping with its interiority but destroys all interiority. An impossible experience and yet real, an impossible experience of the preindividual real, anxiety is "renunciation of the individuated being submerged by preindividual being, which is willingly achieved through the destruction of individuality" (*IPC*, 114; *IL*, 257).

Even though anxiety entails subjective disaster, from its description we may extract "a bit of knowledge," as Michaux would say.[3] In stating that anxiety is "the highest achievement that being on its own can attain as a subject" (*IPC*, 114; *IL*, 257), Simondon affirms two things. First, anxiety is the experience wherein the individual discovers itself as subject by discovering in itself the existence of a preindividual share, which discovery takes the form of violent submersion; second, it entails an experience of substitution: a *lone* subject realizes such an experience, in the absence of any other subject and *owing to* this absence.

If anxiety is the mode of resolution of the tension between preindividual and individuated within the subject, which proves catastrophic *because solitary*, then surely there exists another mode of resolution of this tension, one that is not catastrophic. In fact, for Simondon, anxiety is above all a disastrous substitute for transindividual relation. In the absence of any possible encounter with others, the one who discovers itself to be a subject strives desperately to resolve within it that which exceeds its individuality; it is an attempt bound to fail, whose failure takes the form of a destruction of individuality: we cannot show any more clearly how subjectivity cannot *contain* itself within the limits of the individual.

The Paradox of Transindividual

The experience of anxiety shows that the tension between preindividual and individuated, which a subject may experience within itself, cannot be resolved within the solitary being but only, as we have seen, in relation with others. As we have also seen, this tension is experienced as an incompatibility between the perceptive problematic and the affective problematic. Yet, we learn at the end of the second chapter of the first part of *L'individuation psychique et collective* that "a mediation between perceptions and emotions is conditioned by *the domain of the collective, or transindividual*" (*IPC*, 122; *IL*, 261; emphasis added). The implication is that it is only within the unity of the collective—as a milieu in which perception and emotion can be unified—that a subject can bring together these two sides of its psychic activity and to some degree coincide with itself. But should we conclude from this passage that transindividual is identified with the domain of the collective, as the end of the phrase might lead us to believe? This is not what Simondon suggests in the introduction when he presents the paradigmatic value of the notion of transduction: "to pass from physical individuation to organic individuation, from organic individuation to psychic individuation, *and from psychic individuation to subjective and objective transindividual*"

(*IPC*, 26; *IL*, 33; emphasis added). Why does "transindividual" appear here, precisely where we expect a reference to "collective individuation"? And why is transindividual split in accordance with a subject–object distribution? Such a "split" would not occur if we could establish a simple and pure identity between *transindividual* and *collective*. It remains for us then to understand why Simondon forges this notion of transindividual, making it central to psychic and collective individuation.

After the passage cited above, Simondon declares that the "collective, *for an individuated being*, is the mixed and stable home in which emotions are perceptual points of view, and points of view are possible emotions" (*IPC*, 122; *IL*, 261; emphasis added), and so it is indeed a matter of the collective—not considered "objectively," not from the point of view of the problem of its nature as constituted reality, but considered from the point of view of the psychic problematic, that is, from the point of view of its effects on individuals taking part in its individuation. The nature of this reciprocity between emotions and perceptual points of view is made much clearer a bit further along, when Simondon explains that "Relation to others puts us into question as individuated being; it situates us, making us face others as being young or old, sick or healthy, strong or weak, man or woman: yet we are not young or old absolutely in this relation; we are younger or older than another; we are stronger or weaker as well" (*IPC*, 131; *IL*, 266). It is no longer a matter now of simple perception, because the perceived has become inseparable from the experienced: we feel old *in relationship to* someone younger, weak *in relationship to* someone stronger, and so on.

In Simondon's view, the collective is thus the milieu of resolution of the tension between incompatible subjective problematics arising at the level of the lone subject; but that does not entirely resolve the question of the "relationship" between psychic individuation and collective individuation. In particular, we don't really know in what sense these two individuations can be called "reciprocal"; but it is the notion of transindividual, arising at the intersection of two individuations, which is likely to enlighten us about the nature of this reciprocity. It quickly becomes clear, however, that the "passage" from psychic to collective is not *given* in the form of a belonging of individuals to a community (as ethnic or cultural group), yet neither is it confused with the philosophico-juridical problematic of the passage from civil society to political society through contract or pact: it follows immediately from the thesis whereby the collective results from a specific *operation of individuation*.

A collective is constituted when individuals become engaged in a new individuation, as elements of this individuation. But what conditions the "passage" from psychic individual to collective life? If we recall that it is the tension, lived by the subject, between preindividual and individuated within it, that pushes it to go beyond itself to seek the resolution of this tension, it seems in any case that it is *not only as individuated being* that the subject can be a condition of the collective. But neither does the collective lie within subjects, in the form of an "implicit sociality" that they have only to effectuate. The tendency of individuals to take part in collective individuation cannot by definition be understood as a simple disposition to sociality, as a power to be actualized. Indeed, it is precisely to order to take into account this thorny question of the "passage" toward the collective in terms other than formal mediation or simple actualization of natural power that Simondon forges the concept of *transindividuality*.

As already mentioned, the engagement of a subject in collective individuation occurs as a resolution of the tension within it between preindividual and individuated. What does this mean from the point of view of the subject itself? As experienced by the subject within affectivity and emotivity, this tension may be seen as the form in which the subject is able to perceive the latency of the collective in itself. But this latency is not of the order of a *dynamis* that would aim to become *energeia*; it is the excess of preindividual being manifest within the subject, which is impossible to reabsorb within the individuated being: the individual has to transform in order to arrive at the collective and to individuate the preindividual share that it bears with it.

As such, the tension lived by the subject then appears on the order of a *sign*: a sign of the presence within the subject of a "more-than-individual" aspiring to structure itself. But we must not give in to the teleological temptation of seeing such a sign as a harbinger: for the sign is more a call for a response than an announcement, and in this respect is more like a wave of the hand than a premonitory sign. For the individual to respond to this sign, it will have to pass through an ordeal; transindividual must be discovered, and is only discovered, Simondon tells us, "at the end of the ordeal [that the subject has] imposed upon itself, and which is an ordeal of isolation" (*IPC*, 155; *IL*, 280). Thus a subject cannot encounter transindividual without undergoing an ordeal, that of solitude.

That transindividual, which is the mode of relation to others constitutive of collective individuation, must be discovered and can only be discovered through an ordeal of solitude, therein lies a paradox, to say the least. But it seems impossible to penetrate the "mystery" of transindividual and to learn something of its nature without lingering on the exposition of this paradoxical idea. Simondon finds it exemplified in the encounter of Nietzsche's Zarathustra with the tightrope walker. "Transindividual relation is that of

Zarathustra . . . to the tightrope walker who lies crushed on the ground before him and abandoned by the crowd; . . . Zarathustra feels himself to be a brother of this man, and carries off his corpse to give it a proper burial; it is with solitude, in Zarathustra's being there for a dead friend abandoned by the crowd, that the test of transindividual begins" (*IPC*, 155; *IL*, 280). The ordeal of Zarathustra begins when he realizes that he has tried to speak with other men too soon, and so he isolates himself from them, taking refuge in the mountain where he learns to renounce the sermon and to speak to the Sun. Yet if, as Simondon writes, "the test of transindividuality" begins in solitude, can it really be said that the discovery of transindividual happens "at the end" of the ordeal? Such a conclusion would be entirely right, if the author had spoken of an ordeal *that opens onto* the discovery of transindividuality; but, even though the expression "ordeal *of* transindividuality" may be partly understood in this way, it also tells us something very different; the use of the partitive "of" indicates that what is undergone in this ordeal is not, properly speaking, solitude, but already, through it ("with solitude"), transindividuality itself. And so it is simply our manner of speaking that encourages this sense of the discovery of transindividual happening at the "end" of the ordeal. Yet transindividual is not an end; it is not a transcendent entity to be revealed upon the completion of initiation. As such, if we do not assume that what the subject discovers in the course of the ordeal must already have been sensed by it, we cannot even begin to understand how the subject feels the necessity of an ordeal. This is precisely why the example of Zarathustra interests Simondon: "for it shows us that the ordeal itself is often ordered and initiated by the spark of an exceptional event" (*IPC*, 156; *IL*, 280). For Zarathustra, the encounter with the tightrope walker is the event inaugurating the ordeal: the event is like a spark that spurs the unfolding of the entire process of the constitution of transindividual, but it only happens in isolation. As such, it is only from an exterior point of view that we see in transindividual an end term, and in the event a "revelation": in reality "transindividual is self-constituting" (*IPC*, 156; *IL*, 280), and in a way, solitude is the condition or the milieu of this self-constitution.

In the passage through solitude, which Simondon makes the paradoxical condition for the encounter with transindividual, we cannot help but detect resonance with the other solitary experience already evoked, that of anxiety. These two experiences of solitude are nonetheless so antithetical that they authorize our seeing anxiety as an inverted reflection of the ordeal of transindividuality. The experience of anxiety begins with self-affection of the subject by its preindividual share, and ending—or, it would be better to say, unending—in a catastrophic dissolution of individual structures: it unfurls entirely in the element of solitude, which is but the absence of any other subject. The ordeal of transindividuality, on the contrary, *passes through* solitude as a milieu densely populated with relations. And, in withdrawing from the common relation with others, he who undergoes the solitary experience of transindividuality discovers a relation of an entirely different nature: an encounter (be it the violent and brief one of being in agony) initiates the ordeal of solitude, and the isolated subject confines itself in proximity to an outside (as is the case with this "pantheistic presence of a world subjected to the eternal return"; *IPC*, 156; *IL*, 280). Solitude is no longer an abandonment to be suffered; rather, it comes from a withdrawal, operated by the subject in response to the event, from any relation obliterating the "more-than-individual" carried within it.

The solitary trial of transindividuality cannot be an experience of abandonment, primarily because an actual encounter initiates it. What is extraordinary about this event is nonetheless not the identity of the one who is encountered—it is perhaps for that very reason that, after having evoked Pascal's encounter with the crucified Christ, Simondon takes up the example of the tightrope walker, which he develops at much greater length. The tightrope walker is, in fact, the most ordinary of beings to be found. More precisely: it is only at the moment when the tightrope walker becomes absolutely ordinary, upon the fatal fall that strips him of his quality of tightrope walker, that he may become for Zarathustra the vector of a relation of another type than that linking individuals on the basis of their roles and constituting life in society. The solitude of which Simondon speaks, far from being the suppression of all relations, is rather the consequence of a relation of another nature than interindividual relation, which he names transindividual, and whose establishment calls forth the momentary suspension of all interindividual relations.

But what differentiates interindividual relation from transindividual relation, and why does the constitution of the one require the destitution of the other, however momentarily? In interindividual relation, the individual enters into relation with others and appears to itself in its own eyes as a sum total of social images. This is why Simondon tells us that it is less a matter of a true relation than of a "simple relationship" in which the self is "grasped as a character by way of the functional representation that others make of it" (*IPC*, 154; *IL* 279–280). Still, if the greater part of social exchanges remain satisfied with this sort of relation, this relation does not allow us to grasp the nature of what is to be understood by "collective." The collective is not to be confused with the constituted human community;

it can only happen via that which is neither the constituted individual nor the social as an entity; it arises rather through the preindividual zone of subjects that remains uneffectuated by any functional relation between individuals. The interindividual relationship even constitutes an obstacle to the discovery and effectuation of this residual preindividuality, or at least it provides a cause for avoiding it. This is why only an exceptional event, by suspending the functional modality of the relation to others, and by allowing another subject, stripped of its social function, to appear to us in its more-than-individuality, can force a subject to become aware of what in itself is more-than-individual, and to become engaged in the ordeal called forth by this discovery. Because such an event breaks the functional inter-individual relationship and engenders the necessity for an ordeal, it is, for the subject facing it, *disindividuating*:[4] it provokes a putting into question of the subject that necessarily takes the form of a momentary loosening of the hold of constituted individuality, which is engulfed by the preindividual. Nonetheless, contrary to the catastrophic disindividuation of anxiety in which the individual finds itself destructured in a manner that brings to the surface an indeterminate ground in which all experience is dissolved, transindividual disindividuation is the condition for new individuation.

Now it is clearer how the discovery of transindividual arises from an encounter and demands solitude as a milieu through which to pass. It is only in solitude that communitarian belonging is undone. Still, for the subject to become engaged in the constitution of the collective, first of all, means stripping away community, or at the very least, setting aside those aspects of community that prevent the perception of the existence of pre-individual, and thus the encounter with transindividual: identities, func-tions, the entire network of human "commerce"—of which the principal currency of exchange, as Mallarmé so aptly showed, is language, the "words of the tribe" in their daily usage—which assigns each person to their place within social space.

A Traversal Domain (Subjective Transindividual)

Originating as it does in an unforeseeable event, the failure of the func-tional relation to the other, then, cannot lie in a voluntary decision by the subject. Rather, it is the disindividuating relation to the other that makes a subject able to appear to itself as a subject, that is, as a psychic being truly capable of relation to itself.[5] When the other is no longer encountered on the basis of its function, it becomes that which puts me in question, forcing me to no longer perceive myself through intersubjective representations of sociality. This is why we may say that the psychological individuality of the subject is constituted above and beyond the play of images whereby an individual enters into functional relation with others. Hence "psycho-logical individuality appears as that which is elaborated in elaborating transindividuality" (*IPC*, 157; *IL*, 281). Transindividual relation of subjects among themselves then appears simultaneously to be a self-constituting relation of the subject to itself and to happen through something in the other that is neither role nor function but preindividual reality.

Transindividual is not synonymous with *constituted collective*; but it is not a dimension of the psychological subject separate from the collec-tive, either. Psychological individuality does not preexist readymade, as a condition for the collective—and the collective is not simply constituted of psychic entities. Instead, psychological individuality "is elaborated in elaborating transindividuality," which indicates that the aptitude for the collective, that is, the presence of the collective within the subject in the form of an unstructured preindividual potential, constitutes a condition for the relation of the subject to itself. In effect, the possibility of defining transindividual is strictly tied to the transductive nature of the psychologi-cal subject, which only seems capable of having a relationship to itself (to an "inside") by being turned toward the outside.

If we return to the distinction Simondon introduces between psychic individuation and subjective and objective transindividual, we may now ask what that distinction consists of, and in particular how what he calls subjective transindividual does not become confused with psychic individ-uation. It is doubtless in this respect that the psychic problematic covers an entire series of aspects that do not arise from transindividuality: although a psychic function such as perception finds itself reconfigured by its inscrip-tion in the collective (where points of view become possible emotions), it does not only concern the collective but first and foremost the modality through which a *living* being inscribes itself in the world.

This is why psychological individuality must not be understood as the substantial product of psychic individuation but as the processual result, as the result *in progress*, of what in this individuation is directed toward open-ing the collective; psychological individuality is necessarily constituted at the very center of the constitution of the collective, which explains why "the domain of psychological individuality has no proper space; it exists as something superimposed upon the physical and biological domains" (*IPC*, 152; *IL*, 278). Psychological individuality is constituted as a relation to the physical world and biological world, as a "relation to world and to self," because it is turned as a whole toward the collective: we must thus understand that a separate "psychological world" does not exist, but only, and always already, a "transindividual universe" (*IPC*, 153; *IL*, 279). As such, psychological individuality appears to be essentially *transitional* in nature, covering an ensemble of specific processes organizing the passage from the level due to physical and biological individuation, populated with physical and living individuals, to the level of the collective resulting, as we will see, from an ultimate dephasing of being. This explains why, in Simondon's view, there is no such thing as a constituted psychic reality (something like a "psychological individual") that would constitute the object of a psychological science.

In light of this postulate on the transitional nature of psychic individuality, can we clarify the meaning of Simondon's distinction between subjective transindividual and objective transindividual? Such a distinction may come as a surprise in that it implies precisely the sort of functional division that the philosophy of individuation aims to call into question, and indeed it does not seem to have any other function than calling attention to the two "sides" of transindividuality: the "objective side" of transindividual would be that which is adequate in itself to the description of the constitution of the collective, but transindividual can equally well be apprehended from the point of view of its effects on a subject, under the rubric of "subjective transindividual." Such a hypothesis allows us to take into account the two discussions of the notion of transindividual in *L'individuation psychique et collective*, the first in the section on psychic individuation, and the second in the context of the description of collective individuation. The preliminary distinction between subjective transindividual and objective transindividual subsequently drops out of Simondon's text (probably owing to the inadequacy of these expressions for a reality referring precisely to what escapes both constituted subjectivity and constituted objectivity), and yet it is interesting to see therein a sign of the double-sided aspect that transindividual necessarily presents as a function of the point of view from which we apprehend it.

We will thus speak of subjective transindividual when our aim is to clarify how the elaboration of psychic individuality is transindividual, that is, how *an individual cannot psychically consist in itself*. Indeed it is apparent that what gives consistency to individual psychic life is found neither inside the individual nor outside it, but in what surpasses it while accompanying it, that is, the share of preindividual reality it cannot resolve in itself. Thus, while it is the condition for the collective in the subject (by constituting, as we will see, the basis for objective transindividual), it is also the foundation for psychological individuality: it is impossible to stress this point enough, that it is not relation to self that comes first and makes the collective possible, but relation to what, in the self, surpasses the individual, communicating without mediation with a nonindividual share in the other. What gives consistency to relation to self, what gives consistency to the psychological dimension of the individual, is something in the individual surpassing the individual, turning it toward the collective; *what is real in the psychological is transindividual*. To propose a distinction between subjective and objective transindividual is ultimately to make clear that transindividuality illuminates not only the nature of the collective as reality in becoming, but also the nature of psychic individuality. Thus, to present transindividual on its "subjective" side—as the author of *L'individuation psychique et collective* does in the first part of the work, is to illuminate *in what sense we can be called "subjects."*

The entire paradox of transindividual stems from how, as a process of self-constitution, it necessarily presents itself to us as if coming from without, for it inevitably emerges for us against the ground of interindividual relationships constituting our social existence that are found momentarily stripped away by its constitution. More profoundly, transindividual emerges on the basis of what, in the subject, is not the constituted individual nucleus; "it is in effect at each instant of self-constitution that the relationship between individual and transindividual is defined as what surpasses the individual all the while prolonging it" (*IPC*, 156; *IL*, 281).[6] With this unusual use of capital letters, the author attracts the attention of the reader to the paradoxical topology of transindividual, which "is not exterior to the individual and yet is to some extent detached from the individual" (ibid.). In fact, properly speaking, transindividual is neither interior nor exterior to the individual; it is constituted "at the limit between exteriority and interiority," in this nonindividual zone; it "does not bring [with it] a dimension of exteriority but a dimension of surpassing in relation to the individual" (*IPC*, 157; *IL*, 281).

Insofar as transindividual takes root in this zone of ourselves exterior to the individual, *it wells up in us as if from without*. Yet, as such, the structure of the subject Simondon proposes is closer to a process of subjectification than to a subject conceived as a thinking substance or even as a derived structure (such as Althusser's subject that responds to the call of ideology). It is a subject stripped of interiority because endowed "with an inside that would only be the fold of the outside, as if the ship were a folding of the sea."[7] This inside that presents the greatest relativity—what could be more relative than the "inside" of a fold, which the slightest unfolding is enough to undo—resonates with the relation between exteriority and interiority wherein, Simondon tells us, the point of departure for transindividuality is constituted. From this point of view, the figure of the fold does not seem alien to the model of subjective elaboration that the thinker of transindividuality proposes, even if he defines this elaboration as a double dialectic, "the one interiorizing the exterior, the other exteriorizing the interior" (*IPC*, 156; *IL*, 281). This double dialectic, far from the Hegelian model of logic that Simondon's thought entirely refutes, is without mediation or synthesis. As such, the "domain of transductivity" that is the subject would surely stand to gain by being described in terms of foldings "in the interior of the exterior and inversely," as Deleuze wrote, citing Foucault's words from *Madness and Civilization*.[8]

In one of his later treatments of transindividual, Simondon reaches the point where he states that, since it is a phase of being anterior to the individual, transindividual "is not in a topological relation with the individual" (*IPC*, 195; *IL*, 304). Is this to say that we should avoid topology in describing the nature of the relationship between transindividual and individual? It seems not. At least we need not avoid topology if we take care to specify that it cannot be a matter of a topology governed by categories of *interior* and *exterior*, which are characteristic of a fixed ontology that would obliterate the reality of dephasing. But, taking into account the *anteriority* of transindividual with respect to individual, owing to which their relation may not be understood within the terms of classical topology (the relation of anteriority or exteriority only being conceivable between terms that are situated at the same phase of being), we may hang onto the idea of paradoxical or folded topology. If it is true that a subject is real in that it links an outside and an inside, we will say that what makes for the reality of the subject is the insistence in it of that share of being that came *before* it (that is *pre*individual), and that, as such, is neither inherent nor exterior to it, which we must instead try to conceive of at the limit of inside and outside, or rather *across* them. This share of being traverses the individual—which is why it is called *trans*individual—such that we find it both "on the side" of the subject and "on the side" of the collective, as that which constitutes the reality of psychological individuality as well as the reality of the collective.

The Collective as Process

With the notion of *transindividual*, Simondon is above all proposing a new manner of conceiving what is very inadequately called the relation between individual and society. With that in mind, he is first of all intent on showing that in fact no immediate relation exists between them. This is also why, in his view of things, neither a strictly psychological approach nor a sociological approach can grasp what comes into play in their (non) relationship. Psychologism, which conceives of the group as an "agglomeration of individuals" (*IPC*, 182; *IL*, 297) seeks to highlight within it "psychic dynamisms inside individuals" (*IPC*, 209; *IL*, 312); and inversely, but through a similar procedure, sociologism takes "the reality of groups as a fact" (ibid.). Both approaches entail a similar misunderstanding of the reality of the social, which is neither a substance, that is, one term of a relation, nor a sum of individual substances, but a "system of relations" (*IPC*, 179; *IL*, 295). Individual and society are never in a relationship as one term to another: "The individual only enters into relationship with the social through the social" (*IPC*, 179; *IL*, 295), which is to say, through the relation that each can establish with individuals far distant from it, through the intermediary of a group. In this context, the social appears constituted by "the mediation between individual being and *out-group* [outside group] through the intermediary of the *in-group* [inside group to which the individual belongs]" (*IPC*, 177; *IL*, 294).

Basically, what both psychologism and sociologism misunderstand is that the social *results from individuation*. That which individuates is always *a group*. In effect, a group for Simondon is not a simple assemblage of individuals, but the very movement of self-constitution of the collective; in particular, *inside group* is not for him an entity defined by a sociological belonging, but what "comes into existence when the forces of the future harbored within a number of living individuals lead to a collective structuration" (*IPC*, 184; *IL*, 298). Such an individuation is at once an individuation *of the group* and an individuation *of grouped individuals*, which are inseparable. The group is not constituted by agglomeration of individualities but by "superimposition of individual personalities" (*IPC*, 182; *IL*, 297); these individual personalities do not preexist the individuation of the group, as if they simply happen "to encounter one other and to overlap; the psychosocial personality is contemporaneous with the genesis of the group, which is an individuation" (*IPC*, 183; *IL*, 297), an individuation wherein grouped individuals become "group individuals" (*IPC*, 185; *IL*, 298).

In sum, if psychology and sociology misunderstand the reality of the collective, it is because, when they apprehend it from the angle of the individual or that of society, which are but two polar extremes, both of them forget that this reality consists principally of "relational activity between inside group and outside group" (*IPC*, 179; *IL*, 295). Once again, what is "forgotten" is the reality of the relation, the operation of individuation. And, attentive to the methodological upsets that arose in the mid-twentieth century, Simondon knows that attempts to surpass psychologistic or sociologistic substantialism by choosing an intermediary "microsociological or macrophysical" dimension (*IPC*, 185; *IL*, 299) are bound in advance to fail; for such attempts only make apparent that there is no intermediary "psychosociological" phenomenon to which such a dimension would be adequate. We cannot escape substantialism by objectifying the real in thinner and thinner slices.

But to make the social the site of a specific individuation whereby the relation between individual and society becomes thinkable on a new basis does not happen without difficulties. In particular, what happens, in this perspective, to the idea of "natural" sociality, as much human as animal? How is this natural sociality different from the processual and emergent sociality that Simondon has in mind? The author confronts this question when he explores to what extent we may say that sociality is among the specific characteristics of living beings. He answers that, when morphological specialization makes individuals unsuited to living in isolation (as is the case with ants and bees, for instance) or when the group appears as a mode of behavior for species in relationship with the milieu (as with mammals), we can to some extent consider association as arising from behaviors belonging to species.

But we should not conclude from this that so-called natural sociality is reserved for nonhuman life. Far from hypostatizing an a priori difference between humans and other living beings, Simondon stresses that a mode of natural sociality for humans does exist, that of "functional groups that are like groups of animals" (*IPC*, 190; *IL*, 301).[9] Rather than a distinction between animal societies and human societies, Simondon here establishes a distinction between two modes of sociality: one is situated at the level of "biological, biologico-social, and interindividual relations" (*IPC*, 191; *IL*, 302) and encloses human or animal individuals in their function (or role); the other is called transindividual and displays "potentials for becoming others" (*IPC*, 192; *IL*, 303).

And so there is definitely a natural sociality among humans, a "natural social" that may be defined as "a collective reaction by the human species to natural conditions of life, as through work, for instance" (*IPC*, 196; *IL*, 305). One might think of this first sociality, because it is called *natural*, as arising from infrapolitical association of humans, from what philosophers of law sometimes call the constitution of civil society. But such an approach merely steers clear of what is at stake in the concept of transindividual, which is not orientated toward legitimating the State. And, as we will see, *natural* is not opposed to *political* here. But then, what is the significance of the idea whereby the natural social remains alongside transindividual, while the constitution of transindividual demands a "second, properly human individuation" (*IPC*, 191; *IL*, 302)? And how to understand "properly human"? As he draws a dividing line between natural social and transindividual, will Simondon not be led to hypostatize a substantial human essence in order to explain the existence of a collective conceived as process?

The Being-Physical of the Collective (Objective Transindividual)

In distinguishing transindividual from the sociality that he calls natural, Simondon does not ground his account in an opposition between human and animal, which he refutes; in fact, he makes only the following distinction between human and animal: the human, "having available more extended psychic possibilities, in particular due to the resources of symbolism, more frequently calls on psyche; it is the vital situation that is exceptional in the human, and thus humans feel more destitute. But it is not a matter of a nature, an essence serving to found an anthropology; it is simply that a threshold is crossed" (*IG*, 163, n. 6; *IL*, 165, n. 6). If a difference of nature does not separate humans from other living beings, the "second properly human individuation" constituting the transindividual mode of sociality cannot be defined *in opposition* to animal sociality. Simondon indicates as much in a remark whose discretion does not belie its importance: "In this opposition between human groups and animals groups, I am not setting up animals as truly being what they are, but rather as responding, perhaps fictively, to the human notion of animality, that is, the notion of a being that has relations with Nature governed by species characteristics" (*IPC*, 190; *IL*, 301). We can scarcely oppose the human to the animal because humans share with animals a mode of sociality, precisely what has been defined as a collective reaction of *the species*[10] to the natural conditions of life.

Simondon calls this functional sociality common to human and animals "*natural* sociality," but the choice of terms seems due to a constitutive failure of words. Such a term might lead us to believe that "properly human" individuation, whereby humans go beyond this first sociality, is not "natural." Yet, if "natural" sociality is defined as an ensemble of "relations [with nature] governed by species characteristics," it is thus defined in order to differentiate it from what might be defined as a relation with nature *not governed by species characteristics*. Far from being defined as nonnatural sociality, arising on a plane understood to be that of culture in opposition to nature, the properly human individuation of which Simondon speaks also appears to be a relation to nature, but of another type than the relation of a group of living beings to its milieu. This individuation giving birth to transindividuality is understood neither in terms of an opposition to the animal nor even in terms of an opposition to nature, but as a mode of relation to nature, with the understanding that "Nature is not the contrary of the Human but the first phase of being" (*IPC*, 196; *IL*, 305).

With this reference to nature, Simondon places himself in a pre-Socratic lineage, which is asserted explicitly in his definition of nature as "*reality of the possible*, in the form of this *apeiron* from which Anaximander generates all individuated forms" (ibid.). Properly speaking, nature as *apeiron*, that is, as real preindividual potential, is not yet a phase of being; it only becomes the first phase "after" individuation, and in relationship to the second phase, which is born of the first individuation, and wherein individual and milieu are opposed. Rather, preindividual nature is being without phase. And, as we know, it is not entirely used up in the first (physico-biological) individuation giving birth to individuals and their milieu: "according to the hypothesis presented here, something of *apeiron* remains in the individual, as a crystal retains its aqueous solution, and this charge of *apeiron* may allow it to move onto a second individuation" (*IPC*, 196; *IL*, 305). The second individuation in question here, which reunites the "natures that are borne by many individuals but not contained in the individualities already constituted from these individuals" (*IPC*, 197; *IL*, 305), is that of the collective. All the originality of Simondon's gesture lies in this conception of being as polyphasic, as a function of a nature that is nothing other than real potential. The phases of being are not moments of a process; there is a "persistence of the primitive and original phase of being in the second phase, and this persistence implies a tendency toward a third phase, which is that of the collective" (ibid.).

Individuation of the collective, which gives birth, according to Simondon, to significations, is the second individuation, in the sense that it brings with it a new type of operation, which does not give birth, as the first does, to individuals in relationship to a milieu. From this point of view, physical and biological individuations together constitute a single phase of being, the second. As such, the problem of the "passage" from physical individuation to biological individuation does not have the same meaning as the problem of the passage from biological individuation to collective individuation. The physical individual does not participate in a second individuation in the course of its existence: when a crystal grows, it pursues a single and same physical individuation. The problem of the passage from physical to biological is thus essentially epistemological and concerns the difference between the domain of knowledge of the physical and the domain of the knowledge of the living being. Only living beings sometimes participate in a second individuation in the course of their existence, that of the collective.

With this second individuation, it is already individuated beings, which are subjects insofar as a share of *apeiron* insists in them, that are engaged in a transformative relation. In reuniting the preindividual shares remaining in them, individuals can give birth to a new reality, carrying being toward its third phase. But then why use the language of physics to describe social reality?

It is here that naturalism reveals itself inseparable from the physical paradigm, but then, conversely, this paradigm turns out to be overdetermined by pre-Socratic inspiration. Such reciprocity between natural philosophy and the physical paradigm comes to the fore when Simondon explains that transindividual relation supposes the persistence of a charge of indeterminacy within individuated beings,[11] affirming: "this charge of the indetermined can be called nature," which we must conceive as a "veritable reality charged with potentials actually existing as potentials, that is, as energy of a metastable system" (*IPC*, 210; *IL*, 313).

Thus these shares of nature, of real potential, are what link individuals to one another in the collective; it is because of them that constituted individuals can enter into relation with one another and constitute a collective; these shares are potentials actually existing *as potentials* even though they are not actually structured; they are what is not individuated in individuals. We find, then, at the level of the description of the collective, something we have already seen in the context of relation, namely, that relation "can never be conceived as a relation between preexisting terms but as a reciprocal regime of exchanges of information and of causality in a system that individuates" (ibid.). It is in the context of the collective that Simondon's redefinition of relation best conveys its sense of paradox: far from it being the collective that results from the liaison of individuals founding the relation, it is "individuation of the collective that is relation between individuated beings" (ibid.). The collective is not a result of relation; on the contrary, it is relation that expresses individuation of the collective. For there to be relation, there must be an operation of individuation; there must be a system tensed with potentials: "The collective possesses its own ontogenesis, its own operation of individuation, utilizing the potentials carried by preindividual reality contained in already individuated beings (*IPC*, 211; *IL*, 313–314). What precedes individuals and links them to one another is real:

the operation of individuation reunites these shares of nature charged with potential; consequently, the collective itself "is real insofar as it is a stable relational operation; it exists *physikos* and not *logikos*" (ibid.). That the collective is the site of constitution of significations changes nothing of its "physical" nature—in the sense in which pre-Socratic thinkers are said to be physicians, thinkers of nature, thinkers of the *physis*—; the appearance of signification has a physical condition, an "*a priori* real" (*IPC*, 197; *IL*, 306) borne by subjects.

Owing to this *apeiron* carried within it, a subject does not feel limited to its existence as individual, and "begins to participate by association within its self before any manifest presence of some other individuated reality" (*IPC*, 194; *IL*, 304): therein lies the discovery of transindividual, which can be called "subjective" because it sheds light on the nature of psychological individuality. If we stick to this distinction between subjective and objective transindividual, we would say that objective transindividual concerns the problem of constitution of the collective from shares of nature associated with individuals. It designates the process wherein this reality is structured, "this reality carried with the individual along with other similar realities and carried by means of them" (*IPC*, 194–195; *IL*, 304). Subjective transindividual thus names the effects in a subject of the discovery of its more-than-individuality, of a zone in itself that is revealed to be prepersonal and common.[12] As for objective transindividual, it names the operation in which these "common" shares are collectively structured. But if, as we have already remarked, this distinction drops out of the text, it is surely because it might lead to mistaking objective transindividual for the constituted collective, when objective transindividual simply entails a shift in how we look at the phenomenon of constitution.

The notion of objective transindividual applies to the description of the collective as physical reality. We must stress here that Simondon takes up the problem of the constitution of the collective according to a naturalist postulate, as a natural process, that is, as *real*. Such a gesture avoids any formalist conception of the constitution of the collective by contract,[13] and even any thinking in terms of sovereignty, whose sole concern is to guarantee the legitimacy of the subsumption of society within the State. Consequently, in his inquiry into the real constitution of the collective, Simondon does not, in my opinion, situate himself within a prepolitical thinking about the constitution of civil society (*before* its subsumption within the power of the State), but situates himself in a line of inquiry striving to think the political *outside* the horizon of the legitimization of sovereignty.

If he calls upon a naturalist philosophy to do this, it should nonetheless be clear that nature—that is, what is, by definition, indetermined—appears here as a differentiated reality. *Apeiron*, nature indetermined because still nonstructured, is charged with potentials: *indetermined* is thus not synonymous with *undifferentiated*. Moreover, successive individuations of being do not leave the preindividual unchanged; the share of preindividual nature put to work in collective individuation is something biological individuation has deposited in living beings, but living beings can only gain access to it by *resubmersion* deeper than their vital individuality, for it is a prevital reality. The only term that Simondon has to describe this preindividual is *transindividual*, which creates some confusion to the extent that it designates the preindividual deposited in subjects through vital individuation insisting in them, available for subsequent individuation, as well as its mode of existence as reality structured as collective. But it is possible to resolve this difficulty insofar as it is a matter of referring to something whereby any subject, to the extent that it harbors such a share of uneffectuated nature, is already a collective being, which means that "together, all individuals thus have a sort of nonstructured ground from which new individuation may be produced" (*IPC*, 193; *IL*, 303).

From this naturalist conception of the collective, a philosophical proposition takes shape, which might be called humanist, but implying a humanism constructed on the ruins of anthropology and on the renunciation of the idea of a nature or a human essence.[14] Because belonging to a species is what humans share with other living beings, it is not at the level of species that we can situate the source of Simondon's humanism, his concern for the human. In my opinion, it originates more in the notion that "the human being still remains in evolutionary terms unfinished, incomplete, *individual by individual* (*IPC*, 189; *IL*, 301; emphasis added).

When he evokes human incompleteness "individual by individual," Simondon seems to me, in this aspect of his thought, very far from the hypothesis that sees in the human a being *essentially* incomplete, originarily prosthetic, by nature relying on technical supplementation.[15] Simondon does not speak of the incompleteness of the human in terms of humans in general, but "individual by individual," that is, from the point of view of *each* human insofar as each human is a bearer of potentials, of uneffectuated real possibility. Upon closer examination, then, we ultimately find that Simondon makes such "incompleteness" relative to a positive reality that the human carries with it, its "charge" of preindividual reality, "*reserve of being* as yet nonpolarized, available, awaiting" (*IPC*, 193; *IL*, 303). Thus it is only in consideration of the real potential that humans carry with them "something that can become collective" (*IPC*, 195; *IL*, 304), that *a* human, as a single human, can be considered as incomplete.

Drawing on a statement by Toni Negri about Leopardi, we might say of Simondon's thought that it proposes "a humanism after the death of man,"[16] a humanism without the human to be built on the ruins of anthropology. A humanism substituting the Kantian question "What is man?" with the question "How much potential does a human have to go beyond itself?" and also "What can a human do insofar as she is not alone?"

Scholium: The Intimacy of the Common

The last pages of *L'individuation psychique et collective* present a hypothesis for thinking the collective without invoking a distinction between individual and society. In those pages, individuation of the collective is reexplained via the problem of emotion, whose definition is at the same time clarified. What had until then been called *emotion*—or more precisely "affectivo-emotivity"—which indicated that whereby an individual enters into relation with the preindividual carried within it, now receives the name "emotive latency." When its affective dimension is shaken up, a subject experiences "incompatibility between its charge of nature and its individuated reality [which signals to it] that it is more than individuated being, that it harbors in itself energy for subsequent individuation" (*IPC*, 213; *IL*, 315). But emotion remains latent, only becoming fully effective as transindividual relation within collective individuation, which "can only happen through this being of the subject and through other beings" (ibid.). Properly speaking, emotion coincides so entirely with the very movement of constitution of the collective that we may say, "*there is a collective to the extent that an emotion is structured*" (*IPC*, 211; *IL*, 314; emphasis added). The collective, as Simondon understands it, is born at the same time as emotion is structured across many subjects, as structuration of such emotion.

This reversibility of individuation of the collective and structuration of emotion makes clear that the most intimate of ourselves, what we always experience in terms of inalienable singularity, does not belong to us individually; intimacy arises less from a private sphere than from an impersonal affective life, which is held immediately in common. Before being structured, the collective is, in a sense, already within subjects, in the form of shares of uneffectuated nature, the real potential that insists within each of us. As a consequence, as structured reality, the collective cannot be understood as a residual entity, and its existence merges with the process of structuration of shares of preindividual nature bearing the affective life of subjects. But intimate life cannot be revealed as immediately in common without the collective thereby taking on a molecular dimension. And transindividual ultimately refers to just that: an impersonal zone of subjects that is simultaneously a molecular or intimate dimension of the collective itself.

In his attempt to think constitution of the collective at a molecular level, which is both infraindividual and infrasocial, Simondon moves closer to Tarde, who, for his part, desubstantializes the approach to social phenomena by describing them as processes of imitation. According to Tarde, we never imitate individuals; we imitate flows that traverse individuals, which are always flows of belief and of desire. From this point of view, even invention arises from the imitation of flows, which are conjoined in a new manner *in* the inventor (and not, properly speaking, by him, as if he were the author). We might thus say that an invention is always "a felicitous meeting, in an intelligent mind, of one current of imitation, either with another current of imitation reinforcing it, or with an intense exterior perception making a received idea appear in a new light."[1] Hence the importance that Tarde accords to phenomena of "suggestion at a distance" and "contagion,"[2] which according to him define the mode in which minds can influence one another at a distance simply by virtue of being conscious of the existence of other minds simultaneously in contact with the same ideas (an exemplary case is the public of readers of the same newspaper, and perhaps more exemplary today, the public of television spectators). We find in Simondon a similar interest in phenomena of affective propagation whereby a form is unpredictably precipitated within the social field, considered as a metastable field, as with the propagation of the Great Terror, which may, in his view, be explained through an "energetic theory of the taking on of form within a metastable field" (*IPC*, 69, n. 18; *IL*, 550, n. 5).

Like the theory of invention in Tarde, Simondon's description of the social field, as a field in tension wherein taking on form occurs, proposes a conception of the emergence of novelty in society without recourse to the figure of the exceptional man, a political genius capable of "giving form" to social life. In effect, in a manner reminiscent of the birth of invention from the conjunction of flows of imitation and a series of small differences, which, in Tarde's account, end up producing novelty, Simondon sketches out a social energetics wherein "chance can produce the equivalent of a structural germ" that initiates a transformation of the social field. Indeed, any transformation is produced "by the fact that an idea falls out of nowhere—and immediately a structure arises that spreads everywhere—albeit through some fortuitous encounter" (*IPC*, 63; *IL*, 550). According to

Simondon, such a "human energetics," which focuses on the gap between potentials throwing society into a metastable state, is an indispensable complement to a social "morphology" interested only in the stable structures of social groups. Thus, when we say that the collective is, in a sense, already in subjects, we are adopting the "energetic" point of view on the mode of potentials that may drive individuation of the social field; we should thus think of novelty in terms of collective-in-becoming or (be)coming-collective, and not, especially not, in terms of a preformed structural germ.

Simondon's outline of a human energetics comes in response to a question that long preoccupied him, which he sets forth, before an audience of philosophers and scientists, at the end of a conference held on February 27, 1960, at the French Society for Philosophy: "We would need to ask ourselves why societies transform, why groups are modified as a function of conditions of metastability" (*IPC*, 63; *IL*, 550). How to explain the production of novelty within social reality? Simondon tries to interest his contemporaries in this question, boldly making it the condition for any human science wishing to be rigorous. Yet, to respond to this question supposes an interest in a zone that is neither that of the individual, the object of psychology, nor that of society, the object of sociology, that is, an interest in preindividual interstices left unexplored by either one. Apparently, however, a practice claiming to belong to the "human sciences" cannot venture into these sites without running the risk of losing its status as science at the same time; because, if we follow Simondon's developments and especially his responses to the accusations of objectivism his contemporaries addressed to him, the preindividual zone wherein novelty is produced is prior to both any object and any subject. A human science, to be genuine, should thus become a science of the inobjective—and thus renounce what at first glance appears to define the scientific approach, namely, a domain of objects.

During the debate following the February 1960 conference, Simondon reaffirms the perspective he had developed, insisting that only a "philosophy of nature," that is, a philosophy exploring processes of individuation and situating the origin of all change in a preindividual zone of being, that is, in shares of *nature* associated with individuals, can save us from impoverished conceptions of subject and object. Yet, reading the reactions to his talk today, we notice that most of the interventions are concerned with the status of this philosophy of nature, which is repeatedly conflated with objectivism. First, on the basis of a hermeneutic perspective postulating the primacy of discursive domains, Paul Ricoeur reproaches Simondon for objectifying nature, that is, for not recognizing its discursive reality (its status as signification within a discursive totality). Then he is criticized by Gaston Berger, according to whom, by not starting with consciousness, one necessarily lapses into objectivism, his postulate being that there can only be information for a conscious subject. Only a philosophy of language or of consciousness thus seems able to save us from the danger of objectivism. In response to such objections, it is enough for Simondon to expose the narrowness that inspires them. He first takes up the narrowness of the logicist conception of signification, against which he argues for an understanding of transduction that would transform logic as well as ontology. Thus, to Ricoeur, who stigmatizes "the metaphoric character of all transpositions from the plane of nature to the plane of human significations," Simondon responds that it is not a matter of metaphors, and remarks: "You speak of metaphor because you begin with a conception of significations that does not integrate the notion of transductive relation."[3] Then, in response to Gaston Berger's objection, Simondon underscores the insufficiency of a philosophy of consciousness that does not see that consciousness can be adequately understood only "on the basis of a more primitive trans-consciousness."[4] For Simondon, consciousness individuates on the basis of preindividual nature, at once presubjective and preobjective, that is, prior to the face-to-face relation of subject and object, which results from a process of taking on form. The philosophy of nature to which Simondon lays claim—and this is what seems to scandalize his contemporaries—does not leave room either for philosophy of consciousness or for philosophy of language, or even for anthropology, whose impossibility he here reaffirms in favor of the study of psychosocial "correlations," which alone are real. He could not be clearer. Still, such correlations can only be thought on the basis of the centrality of a preindividual zone of beings, of this share in common with nature in each of them, which is simultaneously the molecular dimension of the collective and the only basis for transformation of societies.

While the author of *L'individuation psychique et collective* is keen on drafting a philosophy of nature, the orientation of his notion of nature is opposed to the notion of nature as "objective" reality, whose description tends ultimately to neglect the subjective reality of consciousness or of discourse. Nature in Simondon is not the objectivist operator of repression of the subject, nor is it opposed to culture or society. This is precisely what seems to "trouble" some of his contemporaries, namely, that Simondon does not pass the baton to anthropology but rather thinks psychosocial reality straight from his philosophy of nature. This is because what he calls "nature" is what renders social transformation thinkable. It is precisely because the philosophy of nature, as he elaborated it, proved adequate to the problem of the appearance of novelty in societies that Simondon chose to move away from the theory of information, which was considered too normative. In fact, his reply to Jean Hyppolite offers an explanation for his choice of a philosophy of nature: "if we were indeed to define a theory of human sciences founded on the theory of Information, we would find that the supreme value is to adapt, to adjust."[5] Against this social ideal of adaptation as the supreme value (the reactualized and stratified version of which today is recognizable in the imperative order-words for professional "insertion" and republican "integration"), Simondon places the emphasis on metastable social states as expressing more profoundly the reality of society: "A prerevolutionary state, this seems to me precisely the type of psychosocial state to study with the hypothesis that I am presenting here (*IPC*, 63; *IL*, 549).

Focusing attention simultaneously on the emergence of novelty in society, and on the impersonal-molecular zone of subjects bearing it, is one node in the philosophy of individuation that proves especially valuable for us today in rethinking the political. Simondon's choice of the term "nature" for the intimate common zone of subjects whereby social change becomes possible seems to me less important in the larger scheme of things than what such a gesture points to—the necessity for making political thought as a whole depend on taking into account preindividual affective life. Simondon's philosophy of nature only makes sense from the angle of the concept of transindividual implied in it, which ultimately expresses nothing other than this disposition toward the collective in each of us, which desubstantializes the collective and makes visible its being as transformation. But there is no doubt that calling it a philosophy of nature has led to misunderstandings.

Between Technical Culture and Revolution in Action

In the context of what it is mistakenly called Simondon's anthropology in designating the part of his philosophy dealing with the collective, the emphasis generally falls more on the evocation of "technical culture" than on the concept of transindividual. This notion of "technical culture," developed especially in *Du mode d'existence des objets techniques* but which returns in the chapters added to *L'individuation psychique et collective*, has greatly contributed to Simondon's reputation as a "thinker of technics." Yet, the systematic foregrounding of this technological image of the philosophy of individuation goes hand in hand with a remarkable silence concerning the "naturalist"[1] side of the theory of the constitution of the collective. Indeed, we can see here *two incompatible tendencies of thought*, two lines leading in such divergent directions that engaging in the one would necessarily amount to betraying the other. But if there is in Simondon's thought a tension resistant to any resolution, if it indeed develops in irreconcilable directions, then we must begin by *situating* its ambiguity.

Toward a "Technical Culture"

The point of departure for *Du mode d'existence des objets techniques* is a crisis, a conflict between culture and technology, born of a misunderstanding of technology on the part of a culture considering technology as a "foreign reality" (*MEOT*, 9) and rejecting it in these terms. "Technical culture" thus gives a name to a manner of thinking that will bear the burden of resolving this conflict, and from the outset, Simondon tells us that only a philosophical manner of thinking can take on the task of rendering culture and technics compatible.

From the opening lines, rather than a "thinker of technics," Simondon appears as a thinker of the resolution of a crisis of humanity in its relation to the world of technics. The reasons for such a crisis seem to reside in the secular opposition between, on the one hand, the world of culture as a world of *meaning*, and on the other, the world of technics considered exclusively from the angle of *utility*. This is why the first sentence of *Du mode d'existence des objets techniques* declares that technical objects are depositories of *sense* or *meaning*,[2] thus attacking the pillar that supports the edifice of discord, and taking on the resonance of a manifesto.

How will philosophy take up the task of revealing such meaning? As is always the case with Simondon, philosophy will remain a philosophy of individuation, an ontogenesis. But what can it mean to think the genesis of technics? Here, as elsewhere, he does not speak of technics in general, but of technical objects, of a multitude of beings resulting from a range of technical operations. The initial aim, then, is to provoke an "awareness of the modes of existence of technical objects" (*MEOT*, 9), that is, to focus not only on their usage, not only on the utilitarian intention that we may project onto them, but also to focus on their genesis. Therein lies the task of a technology seeking to know the functioning schemas of technical objects, not as fixed schemas but as schemas necessarily engaged in temporal evolution. In effect, technical being is invented (which distinguishes it from living being), and yet, precisely because it is invented by living being capable of self-conditioning, technical being is endowed with relative autonomy. This is why, although the *fabricational intention* deposited in the technical object must not be confused with the *utilitarian intention* that is essentially exterior to it, we cannot explain the mode of being of a technical object in terms of the fabricational intention that gave rise to it. Insofar as any technical individual is a system of elements organized to function together and characterized by its tendency toward concretization, we must distance ourselves from human intentionality and enter into the concrescence of technical systems in order to understand the mode of existence of technical objects. With Simondon, we might take up Heidegger's expression (while inverting it) and say that the essence of the technical is truly technical. It does not dwell in a rationality overseeing it, or in a regime of utility it would merely embody. Rather, it consists in this tendency toward ever more concrete solidarity of elements assembled into systems that function, which tendency is autonomous in relation to the act of invention: invention gives birth to a "technical essence" (*MEOT*, 43), that is, to a being that, as soon as it comes into existence, tends to become simplified, and in doing so, engenders a genetic *phylum*, a lineage of ever more concrete technical individuals. An invented technical object cannot attain concreteness all at once, and the ancestor of a technological lineage is necessarily more abstract than the technical individuals coming after it in the same lineage. This is also why the technical object, insofar as it is a system, is not reducible to the scientific system of causal interactions that are applied to it, and always "there subsists a certain difference between the technical schema for the object (which bears the representation of a human finality [which finality requires for its materialization a series of individuals in the same lineage]) and the scientific mapping of the phenomena for which it is the seat (which mapping entails schemas of efficient, mutual, or recurrent causality)" (*MEOT*, 36). As a function of such a tendency of the technical object toward concretization, "even if sciences were not to advance for a certain period of time, the progress of the technical object toward specificity would continue to be carried out" (*MEOT*, 27).

Right at the end of the first of three parts, *Du mode d'existence des objets techniques* arrives at a crucial reformulation of the nature of the crisis of humanity in its relationship to technology, which was put forward quite simply at the beginning. Focusing on the genesis of technical individuals, this part of the work ultimately shows evidence that, from the moment the machine is invented, technical individuality no longer resides in humans, who had until then assumed the role of tool bearers. Inverting the received wisdom to the effect that the machine has "taken the place of man," Simondon explains that it would be more precise to say, "humans have so long played the role of technical individual that, once the machine becomes a technical object, the machine then appears to be human and to take the place of humans, when, on the contrary, it is in fact humans who had provisionally replaced the machine in the period before true technical individuals could be constituted" (*MEOT*, 81). The recent crisis, which takes technics, and more precisely the mechanization of labor processes, to be the source of drama, would thus be due to a misunderstanding of the displacement of the tool-bearing function from human to machine, and as a corollary, a misunderstanding of the liberatory potential such a displacement may possess. Indeed, such a mutation turns out to have positive meaning, if we stop simply applying to technical reality a schema totally foreign to it, which aims to shore up hierarchical distinction between the care brought to the elements of the machine (maintenance, repair, etc.) and the care of organizing ensembles of machines.

This is what Simondon lays out in the second part of the work, in which he brings to light the demand for equality implied by technics in the era of machines. It is a matter of equality between humans belonging to the same technical collective (to which I will return), but first, and more fundamentally, it is matter of equality between humans and machines, which for humans consists in "existing at the same level as machines" (*MEOT*, 125). Existing at the same level as machines affords a possible definition of the "technical life" Simondon attributes to humans insofar as humans are capable of "assuming the relation between the living being that they are, and the machine that they fabricate" (*MEOT*, 125). Because machines know only givens and schemas of causality, it falls back on humans to establish correlations between machines. Although it may appear rather obvious (who would imagine that machines are capable of spontaneously connecting with one another?), this idea takes on new depth in Simondon's version of it. It is as living beings that humans are declared responsible for technical beings, that is, insofar as they are inscribed in time, and as a result, have the capacity to act retroactively on their life conditions by modifying the forms of problems to be resolved. We should recall that it is, in fact, in temporal terms that Simondon explains the capacity to invent, which in his view characterizes living being as a theater of individuation: invention, as the act of a living being "bearing its associated milieu with it," is described as "an influence of the future on the present, the virtual on the actual" (*MEOT*, 58). Thus we might say that the human plays the role of transducer between machines; humans "assure the function of the present, maintaining the correlation, because their life is made of the rhythm of machines surrounding them, which they link together" (*MEOT*, 126). This concern for the correlation of technical beings in relation to one another is what must lead humans to distance themselves from simple consideration of the utility of technical beings, making them "witness of machines . . . responsible for their relation" (*MEOT*, 145). But even if understanding technology well, that is, carefully considering technical objects from the point of view of their mode of being, can contribute to revealing the possibility of a harmonious becoming of humans and technics, nonetheless there are risks coextensive with technology, which Simondon sees actualized in the work of Norbert Wiener: that of the reduction of society to a machine of a particular type. The danger of technicism rears its head, reducing any crisis—even social crises—to a problem of regulation, and presenting as the only ideal, homeostasis, that is, stable equilibrium of attendant forces.

Simondon does not see any other way to avoid technological reductionism but to study, beyond technical *objects*, "the *technicity* of these objects as mode of relation between human and world," which mode must be known "in its relation to other modes of being in the human world" (*MEOT*, 152; emphasis added). The last part of the work is entirely consecrated to this study of technicity, which is the key to understanding what Simondon truly means by "technical culture," which is also where the paradox of normative thinking of becoming starts to appear.

Becoming at the Risk of Teleology

The last part of *Du mode d'existence des objets techniques* assigns to culture the task of bringing together diverse human modes of being in the world that have been progressively sundered. From the time of the division of the world of primitive magic into technics on the one hand and religion on the other, human being in the world has been ceaselessly divided between representational modes (typified by theories and dogmas) and active modes (typified by practices and norms) without truly arriving at a reunification. More than ever, according to Simondon, the cultural function of convergence now falls to philosophy: indeed, what is philosophy for the thinker of individuation, if not genealogy, that is, thinking through genesis, description of becoming? There is no better way of thinking through the unraveling of human modes of being in the world than by carefully retracing the actual process of their separation. It is the task of philosophy to genetically "trace back to" to a moment prior to the rupture of religion and technics into separate entities, even before the rupture between theory and practice. But philosophy is not merely the mode of thought capable of understanding the individuation of human modes of being; and, insofar as it is a mode of thought, philosophy participates in such individuation, taking part in such becoming. Philosophy is, in Simondon's view, the only "force of convergence" for becoming in the long run, and only philosophy can operate this convergence by speaking it: doing it. In other words, "philosophical thought would have the task of taking up becoming once again, that is, of slowing it down in order to *deepen its sense* and to render it more fruitful" (*MEOT*, 213; emphasis added).

Throughout his exposition on the "cultural" role of philosophy, we cannot help but be struck by a recurrent assertion highlighting the existence of a "sense to becoming."[3] And Simondon takes particular care to distinguish his position from finalism[4] and to define becoming as "the operation of a system possessing potentials in reality" (*MEOT*, 155), and these potentials "push" future states into being. In this part of Simondon's study, becoming that entails phases comes to be understood as becoming that is finalized and split into moments. Thus we learn that the "inherence of technicity in technical objects is *provisional*; it constitutes only a *moment* of genetic becoming" (*MEOT*, 157; emphasis added). Is it to bring this all-too-obvious gap back into relation with an immanent philosophy of becoming that the notion of phase is defined nearly immediately after as an "aspect resulting from a doubling of being," in addition to specifying that we must not understand phases in the sense of one "temporal moment replacing another" (*MEOT*, 159)? Everything happens exactly as if Simondon's thinking on becoming were developing, almost on its own, effects that, if pushed to the limit, appear to contradict certain postulates of the study, in particular the antifinalist postulates, which refuse to think becoming as a whole inscribed in time. To avoid finalism, Simondon takes a number of precautions: he takes great care to distinguish the notions of adaptation and equilibrium, which he rejects, from notions of evolution and invention. Thus it is up to humans not to adapt to an environment but rather to invent new structures, to discover "new forms and forces capable of making it evolve" (*MEOT*, 156). But does such a proposition not simply substitute static finalism with evolutionary, dynamic finalism? Such "evolutionism" does not seem to take us far enough from the finalist schema of thought that places ends on becoming.

There is no doubt that, in Simondon's view, becoming is not and cannot be on the order of a simple predetermined actualization of virtualities by means of an end fixed in advance. The direction it takes is definitely not fixed by an end external to it, and the expression "sense of becoming" signifies nothing other than the fact that becoming *in itself* bears meaning or sense. All the work of genealogy lies precisely in reckoning with such sense, bringing it to light and entering into it in order to deepen it; but claiming to transform it would be in vain. This is why simple "theoretical consciousness of [technical] processes" could not be true technical culture; this culture must go to the point of bringing forth the "normative value contained in them" (*MEOT*, 220). Simondon evokes at numerous junctures the necessity for discovering the "values implied in technical realities" (*MEOT*, 149), or "the inherence [in technicity] of values going beyond utility" (*MEOT*, 222). And, we must repeat, the critique of understanding technics in terms of "implementation" is among the most salient ideas of the work. But in order to arrive at an adequate understanding of technics and its constitutive role in human being in the world, is it really necessary to subordinate the genealogical point of view to a normative point of view? Could we not avoid this hypostasis of a "sense of becoming" wherein normativity culminates in the notion of "error against becoming" (*MEOT*, 231)?

The reason for this orientation of Simondon's thinking of becoming seems to me to lie in the regulationist postulate that *Du mode d'existence des objets techniques* takes as its point of departure, casting the elaboration of technical culture as the overall horizon for inquiry. To inscribe speculation within the limits of the notion of culture, with culture in effect defined by its dimension of regulation, of mediation between diverse groups of a society, is to postulate from the outset the resorbable character of any crisis or any conflict that may appear in the course of the inquiry. We are looking, then, for something on the order of a criterion of regulation, or more precisely, for a philosophy that focuses more on values than on norms, a horizon of regulation. Such a goal seems attained with the discovery of "normative value" contained in technical objects. And it is only if culture entails representation adequate to technical realities that it acquires "regulatory normativity" (*MEOT*, 227) in the relation between human to itself and to the world. When all is said and done, it is technics and technics alone, considered from the point of view of its genesis, that contains an intrinsic normativity capable of regulating the social itself, and the role of culture is to make humans recognize this virtual normativity in order for it to become effective.[5]

This normalizing bias to the philosophy of becoming is sufficiently explicit that one may well feel tempted to draw from it a general image of Simondon's thinking. It is not insignificant that Gilbert Hottois, author of the first monograph on Simondon aiming to provide a general introduction to his philosophy, entitled his work *Simondon et la philosophie de la "culture technique"* (Simondon and the philosophy of technical culture). Hottois gears his reading toward the symbolic, ecumenical dimension of Simondon's philosophy to such an extent that he ends up understanding relation exclusively in terms of "rebinding,"[6] that is, as a reality having symbolic efficacy (on the plane of *logos*)—even though Simondon endows it with reality on the order of *physis*.[7] Because Hottois's reading places so much stress on "technical culture," it provides an example in action of the danger of a normative understanding of becoming. There is no doubt that, in declaring that Simondon's ethics can be summarized in terms of "having-to-become,"[8] and claiming that its essence lies in including "having-to-be" within being-in-becoming, Hottois goes well beyond what is actually written in Simondon's text; yet, at the same time, he reveals a certain tendency within Simondon's thought. In other words, we might say that, while Simondon has renewed the thinking of being by substituting being-in-becoming (being that is only its becoming) for being understood as substance, he has not totally rid his philosophy of a substantialist conception of ethics in the form of having-to-be; he has simply displaced having-to-be onto having-to-become. Indeed, when we strive to render the norm immanent, we run the risk of effectively normalizing immanence.

A Physical Ethics of Amplification and Transfer

Attention has often fallen on an obvious tension in Simondon's thought between two tendencies or orientations: an ecumenical tendency that aims for the symbolic unification of the diverse, and another, which I have called naturalist, that focuses on the emergence of novelty from the pre-individual. But it seems to me that nothing justifies reducing the second orientation to "mystico-poetic philosophy," as Hottois does.[9] The motivation implicit in Hottois's reading is polemic engagement with so-called philosophies of difference, yet Hottois remains content with an opposition between the unbound multitude and "rebinding," between the different and the reassembled. Consequently, his account completely shuts out what exceeds such a play of oppositions within Simondon's thinking of a more-than-individual center of being.

It is instructive in this regard to spend a bit more time on the conclusion of *L'individu et sa genèse physico-biologique*. While essentially identical with *L'individuation psychique et collective*, these concluding pages nonetheless include some significant modifications. Simondon asks if a theory of individuation can "through the intermediary of the notion of information offer an ethics" (*IG*, 242; *IL*, 330), and he poses this question immediately after having recalled that information is, in his view, nothing other than the internal resonance of a system in the process of individuating, the power radiating between one domain of individuation and another (*IG*, 240–241; *IL*, 328–329). The very terms of the question lead the author to a definition of ethics wherein ethics does not reside in fixed norms but in values that are "the preindividual of norms" (*IG*, 244, n. 14; *IL*, 332, n. 14), that is, in the capacity of norms to mutate under the pressure of becoming, or even more, "the capacity for an amplifying transfer contained in the system of norms" (*IG*, 243; *IL*, 331). Throughout this passage, this notion of "amplifying transfer," which defines value in terms of a sense of relativity immanent to norms, also comes to characterize the ethical subject. The notions of "transfer" and "amplification" appear in six of the seven notes added by Simondon to this version of the conclusion, as well as in all of the corrections that he makes to the main text;[10] coming so close to the end of the text, these modifications as a whole seem intended as an insistent reminder of the physical character of the ethics stemming from the theory of individuation. In these pages, in effect, we can no longer distinguish between the level of sense or meaning and that of *physis*. And while ethics is said to be "sense of individuation," and there is ethics only "to the extent that there is information, that is, signification" (*IG*, 245), ethics is simultaneously apprehended as reticular reality, the capacity to link the preindividual in many acts: "Ethical reality is indeed structured in a network, that is, acts take on resonance in relation to one another . . . within the system they form, which is becoming of being" (ibid.). Yet: "Acts are in a network to the extent that they are *taken over a natural ground*, a source of becoming through continued individuation" (*IG*, 247; *IL*, 335; emphasis added). The ethical act, then, is one that "contains in itself a power of amplification" (*IG*, 246, n. 16; *IL*, 334, n. 16), rendering it capable of entering into relation with other acts, to the extent that they may be said "to contain" preindividual. This relation "goes from one act to others in the same way that one may go from yellow-green to green and to yellow through augmentation in the amplitude of the band of frequencies," linking acts that have "lateral bands" and are said to radiate (ibid.). From this perspective, we are not surprised to learn that "the value of an act is its amplitude, its capacity for transductive spacing out" (ibid.). And insofar as preindividual, that is, the reserve of being from which everything becomes, is defined *physeos*, how could it be otherwise?

In such an ethics, the subject lives on by affirming its relative character, or more precisely, its relational character, by inscribing its acts into the network of other acts as much as it can. But this inscription is not simple integration, and relation can no longer be reduced to rebinding on the order of logos: for the power of amplification defining any ethical act exceeds the simple relation of harmony between members of a community. To act ethically, for a subject, means in effect to be affirmed as a "singular point in an open infinity of relations" (*IPC*, 254; *IL*, 506), that is, to construct a field of resonance for other acts or to prolong one's acts in a field of resonance constructed by others; it is to proceed on an enterprise of collective transformation, on the production of novelty in common, where each is transformed by carrying potential for transformation for others. This, then, is the definition of collective individuation, opening into the dimension of transindividual.

Clearly then, it is impossible to separate out what Hottois calls "rebinding" and hold it apart from this other side of Simondon's philosophy describing the preindividual dimension of being that Hottois styles as "mystico-poetic." On the contrary, if an act is all the more symbolic when it has greater power of amplification and resonates with the greatest number of other acts with which it constitutes a network, then the power of symbolic relation between acts would seem to ensue from the central preindividual zone of being, from the "ground of nature" of which Simondon speaks. In these pages, Simondon establishes that the reticular inscription of acts alone provides the criteria for their value, and affirms the immanence of an ethics of becoming, and thus we may read them in counterpoint to the teleology of technical culture that arises when "sense of becoming" is hastily hypostatized. Indeed it would seem that what allows us to escape the universality of technological normativity is the thematization of reticularity at the heart of Simondon's thinking of technics.

Hylomorphism versus Networks

"The act is neither matter nor form" (*IG*, 246; *IL*, 334). Such a statement serves to firmly establish the difference between understanding ethics as reticular reality, which in Simondon's view is the only way adequate to the theory of individuation, versus hylomorphic conceptions that see in ethics a system of norms functioning as a priori forms imposed upon action from without. Simondon explains, "Ethical reality is indeed structured in a network, which is to say, there is resonance of acts in relation to others, not through their implicit or explicit norms, but directly within the system they form, which is becoming of being" (*IG*, 245; *IL*, 333). Reticularity, which is the condition for immediate resonance of acts within structuration of potential in common, is what takes us from a normative horizon to a horizon of amplification of action. Fidelity to the sense of becoming is here subordinated to transductive spacing out of acts in networks, where the network is not the means of the act but its milieu.

Similarly, in *Du mode d'existence des objets techniques*, the notion of reticularity allows Simondon to go beyond a simply normative point of view, but here reticularity designates networking not of acts but of techniques. While it is true that, at one level, Simondon grants intrinsic normativity to technical objects independent of any social normativity,[11] it is only by passing through the level of technical *objects* to the deeper level of *technicity* that we can grasp what normativity inherent in technics consists in (because "technical objects result from an objectification of technicity; they are produced by it, but technicity is not exhausted in objects and is not entirely contained in them either"; *MEOT*, 163). And what we discover then is not a system of technical norms but, here as well, a mode of being that exceeds each technical object taken separately, namely, reticularity. As such, while there is indeed "normative value" in technics, above and beyond technical individuals, it belongs to "the world of plurality of techniques" and consists in "technical reticulation of concrete ensembles" (*MEOT*, 220). The reticular character of the organization of techniques confers on the technical world a capacity to condition human action as such. And indeed, confronted with a network, we have no other choice than to keep our distance, or, on the contrary, to "join up with the network, adapt to it, participate in it" (*MEOT*, 221). Although we may change tools or construct a tool ourselves, "we cannot change networks or construct a network ourselves" (ibid.). This is in fact the key point in understanding why technics cannot be understood as a simple means for action. Characterizing technicity in terms of reticularity is what allows us to make a radical break with the description of technics based on the category of means, and in sum, to break with the schema of utility, which is suited only to the tool. Here, too, reticularity (of integrated technical ensembles) is opposed to hylomorphism (of the tool). And the schema of the network, antithetical to that of hylomorphism, seems, in Simondon's view, even to constitute a weapon against it, affording a possibility for escaping the hylomorphic mode of thought and action.

At stake is nothing less than the relationship between thinking technics and thinking the collective in the work of Simondon, and so, if we aim to fully expunge this sense of normative value attributed to technicity, it is worthwhile looking closely at the thesis Bernard Stiegler develops in his ambitious work, inspired by Simondon.[12] Apparently Simondon is an important source of inspiration for Stiegler, because Stiegler closes his general introduction to the work saying, "Simondon, with his analysis of psychic and collective individuation, allows one to conceive through the concept of 'transduction,' an originary constitutivity of temporality—without Simondon adopting such a conception himself."[13] Upon establishing that his thesis is permitted but not presented clearly by Simondon, Stiegler reformulates the "originarily techno-logical constitutivity of temporality" through the idea that "technogenesis is structurally prior to sociogenesis,"[14] which Stiegler grounds in the hypothesis of continuity between *Du mode d'existence des objets techniques* and *L'individuation psychique et collective*, which continuity, for all that it is obvious, was apparently not set forth by its author. According to Stiegler, although Simondon never actually states it as such, technics occupies a constitutive place in psychic and collective individuation. Simondon's silence, however, seems to me more indicative of an intellectual choice than theoretical blindness. And despite drawing inspiration from Simondon, Stiegler's reading seems to advance an interpretation of Simondon's thought that evacuates the specificity that Simondon accords to individuation of the collective.

There is indeed in Simondon the idea of normativity to technics. But Simondon's idea distinguishes between, on the one hand, normativity contained within *technical objects* independently of social normativity, which may even become the source of new norms in a "closed community" (*IPC*,

264–265; *IL*, 513), and on the other hand, normativity of reticular organization *of the technical world* as conditioning *human action*. For his part, Stiegler
hammers out the idea of univocal normativity of technics *as such*, for what
he calls "socio-genesis." If the concept of socio-genesis cannot, however,
be found in Simondon, it is surely because such a concept amalgamates
notions that refer to different problems, notably, notions of community,
society, and psychic and collective individuation. All nuance expressed in
Simondon's differentiation of these notions is in Stiegler flattened into the
idea of reappropriation of technical becoming by society.

Following Stiegler's hypothesis, we might conclude that "technics is
invention, and invention is novelty," and everything is a matter of "adjustment" between "technical evolution" and "social tradition," even if such
adjustment does not happen without "moments of resistance, since technical change, to a greater or lesser extent, disrupts the familiar reference
points in which all culture consists."[15] When the thematic of *social transformation* is used to foreclose that of *cultural evolution*, all the specificity
of collective individuation is eradicated. In this way, the hypothesis of an
advance of technogenesis, which subordinates psychic and collective individuation to technical evolution, constrains the production of novelty to
technical invention. Properly social invention seems unthinkable within
the framework of such a hypothesis. Yet, as we have seen, when Simondon
inquires into the reasons for transformation of societies (see, e.g., *IPC*, 63;
IL, 549), his answer is not structural advance in technics but the existence
of shares of preindividual nature associated with individuals who, because
put in common upon *specific individuation of the collective*, give birth to
transindividual. As such, while it is true that the problem of connecting
Du mode d'existence des object techniques with the rest of Simondon's work,
especially with *L'individuation psychique et collective*, is without a doubt one
of the crucial problems posed in the context of Simondon's thought, it
seems illegitimate to make technical invention the basis for all production
of novelty in being, and in particular, the basis for all social transformation.

If we adopt Stiegler's perspective, we would not be able to account for
what, in the human, tends to go beyond the present state, which imparts
"movement to go always farther," to cite an expression of Malebranche
that Simondon quite likes, by postulating the constitutive incompleteness
of the human. To declare "All supplement is technics"[16] is to completely
overdetermine in technological terms the powers of human being. Such a
declaration follows logically from the postulate whereby mortals are said
to share "an originary *default* of origin that opens like a default of community, the community of a default."[17] While he thoroughly stigmatizes

those who "do not accept that . . . humans are prosthetic beings,"[18] Stiegler does not seem to countenance the possibility that *humans share more than default* or lack. Yet such a possibility seems to me to be the lesson to draw from Simondon's hypothesis on the existence of preindividual potential associated with individuals, on their common belonging to an ontological dimension preceding them; and nothing in it forces us to conceive of preindividual as technological. If human individuals should not be conceived on the basis of fixed bioanthropological nature, I do not see why they should be conceived on the basis of original defect that we then take pains to call originary in entirely metaphysical nostalgia for foundations.

Even when philosophy strives to be antiessentialist and deconstructivist, it seems condemned to an abstract point of view on the human, at least as long as it does not see that the basis for human living is becoming—for the question is less to know what *defines* human than to know what *makes for its becoming*—that is, real preindividual potential that, because prephysical as well as prevital, cannot be conceived of as biological any more than it can be conceived as anthropological, since it is what is prehuman in humans. And so, as a function of this concept of potential, we can even try to invert Stiegler's procedure, and rather than deducing an uncertain "politics of memory"[19] from technological advance, we may ask if life itself is not always already political, if "the political is [not] already contained in life as its most valuable kernel."[20] In my view, it is such a political "kernel" within human life that Simondon brings to light when he describes psychic and collective individuation as emotion structuring itself (*IPC*, 211; *IL*, 312–313). And we would look in vain within his thought for a ground for the political existence of humans if we look anywhere but in shares of *apeiron* that are never fixed, arising within subjects in whom they insist throughout their affective life, and as a function of which any collective individuation wherein a subject is constructed begins with disindividuation.

We can now better understand Simondon's gesture of seeking to renew human action through engagement with reticularity of connected technical ensembles. In such reticularity, Simondon sees, in effect, the possibility of finally escaping the hylomorphism characterizing the phase of being in the world to which we still belong, and into which we have entered by breaking the "vital liaison between human and world" that characterized "primitive magical unity" (*MEOT*, 163). Yet, when he writes, "The powers, forces, and potentials compelling action exist in the reticular technical world as they might have existed in the primitive magical universe" (*MEOT*, 221), Simondon does not for all that qualify this primitive mode of being in the world as *already technical*. And he does not conflate preindividual with a being-prosthetic of the human, for, owing to shares of *apeiron* associated with it, preindividual is, on the contrary, precisely what is deposited in technical beings in the course of their act of invention. Because he avoids hypostatizing technicity by making it originary for the human, Simondon tends to articulate the powers and forces of today's technical world in terms of what humans, as beings with potential, can do. And that is what leads him to see in the contemporary technical world, *as reticular reality*, the milieu offering the possibility of reconstructing a relation to the magical unity of the *analog* world, which relation was not fusion of human and world, but "reticulation of the world into privileged sites and privileged moments" such that "all the power of action of humans and all the capacity of the world to influence humans are concentrated in these sites and moments" (*MEOT*, 164). Beyond the hylomorphic scission of action that was imposed by the age of the tool, what interests Simondon is not to rediscover this magical relation to the world, which was characterized by a reciprocal influence of human and world wherein humans could "enter into a relation of friendship with it" (*MEOT*, 166), since this relation is definitively lost to us; but *through* the contemporary technical network, we might come to construct a new modality of relation, a modality of transductive relation of human to nature and transindividual relation between humans.

Toward a Revolution in Action: Transindividual against Labor

In *Du mode d'existence des objets techniques,* Simondon is trying to pave the way for a transformation of our relation to technics, which naturally leads him to an analysis of what he calls "alienation of humans in relationship to the machine" (*MEOT*, 118). The novelty of his analysis consists in noticing a "psycho-physiological" dimension to this alienation, which he sums up by saying that "the machine no longer prolongs the corporeal schema" (ibid.): humans, accustomed to playing the role of tool bearer, find themselves in a situation of disadaptation vis-à-vis the machine when machines begin assume that function. This observation leads Simondon to call for the establishment of a new relation to machines, which would no longer consist only in serving them or commanding them. Above and beyond the role as assistant to or commander of machines, "the human can be coupled with the machine as equal to equal, as a being that participates in its regulation" (*MEOT*, 119–120). We must go beyond the cultural task of "raising philosophical and notional awareness of technical reality" through an existential ordeal in which all human beings ought to take part, that of "taking on a particular position in the technical network" (*MEOT*, 228), whereby each would have the experience, as a participant, of a series of processes in which humans and machines are inextricable.

As Simondon himself admits, the call for a transformation of our relationship to technics cannot be achieved entirely at the cultural level of representations but would imply social changes. It is especially in the conclusion of *Du mode d'existence des objets techniques* that he sets forth these indispensable changes that would summon forth an adequate understanding of technicity, and *the suppression of work* figures in the first order of changes: "Work should become technical activity" (*MEOT*, 251–252). He does not leave us in the dark about the critical and utopian correlates of this demand. As such, he lucidly criticizes the inadequacy of the organization of work within the Fordist capitalist enterprise for egalitarian aspirations of technical becoming: "The alienation of the worker results in a rupture between technical knowledge and its conditions of use. This rupture is so pronounced that, in a great number of modern factories, the role of regulating the machine is strictly separated from that of using the machine, and workers themselves are forbidden to regulate their own machine" (*MEOT*, 250). This logically leads Simondon to remark—in an offhand manner in sharp contrast with the bold "utopian" character of his observation—that we "should be able to discover a social and economic mode in which the user of the technical object would be not only the owner of the machine but also the one who chooses and maintains it" (*MEOT*, 252).

But how exactly does this passage analyzing the inadequacy of our relationship to technics bring about the formulation of properly social critique? If we judge by the scant interest in this aspect of Simondon's theory within existing readings of our so-called thinker-of-technics, there seems no direct path from the one to the other. And yet, the concluding pages are not ambiguous at all on this head.

All of the *utopian* considerations cropping up in the conclusion to the work follow directly from critical analysis of labor as the privileged site of human alienation in relationship to the machine, which has led to human alienation becoming the site for analysis of technics in general; but such an approach can easily lead to a series of misunderstandings.

For his part, Simondon sees in labor the origin of the hylomorphic schema. In his view, the hylomorphic schema "represents the transposition into philosophical thought of the technical operation drawn from labor and taken as the universal paradigm for the genesis of beings" (*MEOT*, 241). In Simondon's genealogy of modes of being in the world, this phase of human action appears when the unified magical mode splits apart and gives birth to religion and technics, and now it is a matter of the individual impressing a "form-intention" that is of human, not natural, provenance, upon "matter to be worked" (*MEOT*, 242). As such, in labor, humans work and achieve the operation of taking on form through the intermediary of their bodies, gesture by gesture, yet remain necessarily blind to the operation of which they are nonetheless the operator: thus, in the encounter with matter on which the worker must impose form, "the worker must keep his eyes fixed on the two terms to be joined together (such is the norm of work), not on the complex internal operation through which this joining is obtained" (ibid.). It is the very essence of labor to blind the worker to what is central to the operation being carried out. Labor can thus be defined as that modality of technical operation "that *imposes form on passive and indeterminate matter*" (*IG*, 49), and in this sense it reflects the sociohistorical situation that gave birth to it: slavery. "It is essentially the operation commanded by the human and executed by the slave," explains Simondon, adding, "The active character of form, the passive character of matter, respond to conditions of transformation into a social order that assumes hierarchy" (ibid.). Thus, form is essentially a depository for the order expressed by the one who commands labor. This inspires Simondon to say some pages later in the very beautiful opening of *L'individu et sa genèse physico-biologique* that "form is neither logically nor physically generic, but socially: a single order is given for all bricks of the same type" (*IG*, 55; *IL*, 57), or for all the planks that we would like to extract from a multiplicity of different tree trunks.

The genealogy that Simondon proposes for labor as a modality determined sociohistorically by a technical operation that illegitimately sets up a "universal paradigm for the genesis of beings" (*MEOT*, 242–243) immediately extends into *radical critique* of labor, formulated in a manner equally distant from the Marxist perspective and from that of psychologists of work. For Simondon, labor is alienating in essence. We thus understand why it would be illusory to seek psychological solutions for the problems arising within labor communities: "The problems of work are problems related to alienation caused by work, . . . alienation that is essentially due to how individual being is situated within work" (*MEOT*, 249). But elsewhere, Simondon's critique does not bear only on the capitalist situation, for in his opinion, "we may define a precapitalist alienation that is essential to work as such" (*MEOT*, 248). The alienation of which Simondon speaks is thus in his view more fundamental than what he designates as "the economic aspect of alienation" (*MEOT*, 249), which he attributes to analysis in the manner of "Marxism." Indeed, this point is apparently of some importance to him, since he evokes it at many junctures throughout the work.

He develops it notably by saying that alienation "seized by Marxism as having its source in the relationship of the worker to the means of production does not arise only . . . from a relationship of ownership or of nonownership between the worker and the instruments of work" (*MEOT*, 117); alienation "appears at the moment when the worker is no longer owner of his means of production yet it does not occur only because of severing the link to ownership" (*MEOT*, 118). As such, if we demur, on the one hand, that Marxian thought, however relative such a thing may be, is absolutely not economism, then we also see, on the other hand, that, at the very moment he critiques Marx, Simondon is far closer to him than he thinks.

While it is true that Marx often relies heavily on the analyses of economists, we must recall that he consistently defines his own project in terms of "critique of the political economy," which critique aims to make apparent the mystifying character of the point of view of economists, since, under capitalism as a specific relationship of production, the economy—all that concerns the analysis of surplus-value, profit, production of wealth, and so on—becomes inseparable from politics—that is, social relationships of domination by means of which capital constrains living labor to become objectified labor within the commodity. Nonetheless, in its concern to propose global comprehension of human action and to explain the relations between humans and nature, such an analysis does not entail economism. Thus, when Marx declares that "the short-sighted behavior of humans vis-à-vis nature conditions the short-sighted behavior between them, and . . . the short-sighted behavior between them conditions in turn their short-sighted relationships with nature,"[21] he proposes an analysis of the relation of humans to nature and of their mutual relation that is resonant with Simondon's later one. In particular, this passage by Marx recalls the critique that Simondon addresses to the project of technocratic domination of nature, within which "The machine is only a means; the end is the conquest of nature, the domestication of natural forces by means of a first servitude: the machine is a slave that serves to make other slaves" (*MEOT*, 127). And, we may say that, in Simondon as well, it is because domination is first by humans over nature (as bearers of form upon matter conceived as amorphous) that it can turn into domination by humans (as owner of materials and master of forms) over humans (as laborers who reunite the two through their work, that is, through their muscular energy). It thus seems to us important to try to understand why Simondon wished to see a strictly economist point of view in Marxian analyses, while in fact he never cites from them but evokes them through signifiers such as "Marx" or "Marxism."

When he speaks of the insufficiency of economic critique of alienation, Simondon seems to want to stigmatize a mode of thought that in his view does not get to the deepest sources of alienation. As such, it would be fairer to say that Marx simply does not situate alienation in the same place that Simondon does. Whereas Simondon sees it in the inadequate relationship that humans, incapable of overcoming the dialectic of domination and submission, maintain with machines, Marx situates it at the level of relationships of production as an inextricable mixture of exploitation and domination. Between the short-sighted behavior of humans toward nature and their short-sighted behavior toward one another, Simondon posits their misunderstanding of the machine and of the equality that it requires, their inadequacy to technicity, as that which prevents any fair relationship to nature and among them; for Marx, on the other hand, what comes between the two are social relationships of production, whose inequality structures the material life of humans.

Simondon apparently needed to reduce the Marxian point of view to economism in order to formulate his hypothesis of a more general alienation than the one situated on the economic level, which hypothesis does not seek to deny the existence of economic expropriation but seeks to resituate it in the right place. Even though Simondon himself clearly shows the sociopolitical reality of domination (for instance, p. 49 of *L'individu et sa genèse physico-biologique*), it nonetheless becomes relativized through this operation of localization, taking a somewhat tenuous place in the economy of Simondon's discourse. In announcing, for instance, that "the servile condition of the worker *has contributed to obscuring* the operation whereby matter and form were forced to coincide" (*MEOT*, 242; emphasis added), Simondon suggests that the social situation of hierarchy is not essential to understanding the nature of labor, which appears to contradict the passages in *L'individu et sa genèse physico-biologique* previously cited. This seems all the more surprising because Simondon never loses sight of the fact that, especially from the time when a role auxiliary to machines was imposed upon humans, *human* takes on two senses or orientations, as manager and as worker, or rather as engineer and as laborer carrying out orders. Still, although he shows awareness that this properly social dichotomy is a function through which the "human who thinks of progress is not the same as the one who works" (*MEOT*, 116), and due to which the engineer and the user do not have the same sort of technical experience, Simondon continually returns to a denunciation of the alienation of the human *in general*, which sometimes takes the form of "back to back" dismissals of dominators and dominated in light of their equally alienated situation vis-à-vis technicity. It is thus that bankers are said to be "as alienated in relationship to the machine as members of the new proletariat are" (*MEOT*, 118).

From this point of view, any event, and in particular any social conflict entailing an attack on technics as one of its aspects, can only appear to Simondon as a misunderstanding of the intrinsic normativity of technics, as an essentially reactionary nostalgia for the *human*-tool-bearer dispossessed of that role: "The frustration of humans starts with the machine that replaces them, with the automatic loom, with the forging presses, with the equipment of the new mills; these are the machines that the worker will shatter during riots, because they are his rivals, no longer motors but tool-bearers (*MEOT*, 115). Passing as he does in the same phrase from the human as generic subject of alienation in relationship to the machine, to the worker as specific incarnation of the misunderstanding of machines, Simondon does not attribute any specific value to the point of view of workers about machines. At no moment does he ask himself if the violent reactions of workers in their encounter with machines do not express something about their relationship to technics other than a simple blindness to becoming. With respect to movements like that of the Luddites in England (from 1811 to 1817) or that of the Canuts in Lyon around 1830, he thus adopts the position that E. P. Thompson, in his meticulous study of Luddism, presents as the most common position, which consists in seeing in it "an uncouth, spontaneous affair of illiterate handworkers, blindly resisting machinery."[22] And, in his detailed analysis of the Luddite movement that drew its name from a certain mythic General Ludd to whom the principal members of the movement—croppers, framework-knitters, and weavers—claimed allegiance, Thompson nicely shows that such a struggle did not express rejection of the introduction of technics *in general*. What the workers who smashed machines (which happened more frequently during organized nighttime raids than in the context of riots) opposed was especially "the encroachment of the factory *system*."[23] Thus Thompson underscores that, during the year 1811, in Nottingham and Yorkshire, only those frames producing piecemeal work at low prices were destroyed, as the Nottingham Review, a radical journal of the middle classes, noted at the time: "Machines, or *frames* . . . are not broken for being upon any new construction . . . but in consequence of goods being wrought upon them which are of little worth."[24] According to Thompson, the organized destruction of machines was thus more indicative of refusal of deskilling of the labor force brought about by large-scale production than refusal of machines per se. What the workers rejected was the miserable and constrained way of life being imposed on them. Certainly, the Luddites found refuge in the customs of their trade and expressed nostalgia for a way of life about to disappear; but, as Thompson shows, they tried especially "to revive ancient rights in order to establish new precedents. At different times their demands included a legal minimum wage; the control of the 'sweating' of women or juveniles; arbitration; the engagement by the masters to find work for skilled men made redundant by machinery; the prohibition of shoddy work; the right to open trade union combination."[25] Thus, a slight shift in emphasis is enough for what looks to Simondon like blindness and misunderstanding about the true nature of machines to appear instead as clairvoyant at another level. Provided, of course, that we wish to recognize the existence of an experience of technics specific to workers, whose relationship to machines would not occur without an oppressive global system. And it is hard to understand why, even though Simondon deplores the fact that the machine is only apprehended in work as means, he never takes into account the specific experience of technics following from labor, an experience such that the worker goes into the factory not as *human* but as part of mutilated humanity.

Nevertheless, Simondon never ceases to insist that only a definitive departure from the paradigm of labor can permit humans to transform their inadequate relation to technics, to nature, and to one another. The leitmotif with which *Du mode d'existence* concludes could not be clearer in this respect: Simondon says that *the technical operation is not reducible to labor*, and thus, to be faithful to the essence of the technical operation, "labor must become technical activity" (*MEOT*, 251–252). It is only on the basis of technical activity that the relation of humans to nature and of humans to one another can be reinvented. Indeed, technical activity appears as the mode of relation to the technical object linking these two relations in new ways.

On the one hand, in effect, technical activity "reconnects humans to nature with far richer and better defined linkage than that of the specific reaction of collective labor. A convertibility of human into natural and of natural into human is established through technical schematism" (*MEOT*, 245). Thus, when the technical object is put into action in conformity with its essence—that is, not as a means, a tool, or implement, but as a functioning system inscribed within a network of machines to which it is connected—it becomes the site for a new relationship to nature, no longer a utilitarian relationship mediated by the organism of human individual, but a relationship of immediate coupling of human thought to nature.

On the other hand, Simondon claims that "technical activity . . . is the model for collective relation" (*MEOT*, 245), and relation to the technical object can only become adequate "to the extent that it succeeds in bringing this interindividual collective reality into existence, which we call transindividual because it creates coupling between the inventive and organizational capacities of many subjects. There is relation of reciprocal causality and conditioning between the existence of distinct, nonalienated technical objects that are used in a nonalienating manner, and the constitution of such a transindividual relation" (*MEOT*, 253). Beyond the simple interindividual relation such as it exists in the labor community in particular, the technical object adequately understood and put to work can allow for the emergence of transindividual.[26] Ultimately, then, Simondon discerns the "true way to reduce alienation" (*MEOT*, 249) in "transindividual collective" as an amplifying mode of relation between humans, which is the flipside of nonservile relation to nature. As his commentators have often noted, reducing alienation means showing that technical objects are not the Other of the human, but themselves contain something of the human: the "object that comes of technical invention carries with it something of the being that produced it" (ibid.). But it is crucial to understand that what technical invention carries *is not what is specifically human in the human*; it is "this charge of nature that is conserved with individual being, and which contains potentials and virtuality" (ibid.); this is the very charge from which transindividual is constituted. Thus, in a general manner, insofar as transindividual is born from individuation in common of shares of preindividual reality associated with individuals, when there is invention, it is really a modality of transindividuality constituted through the intermediary of preindividual share deposited in the technical object: the invented technical object becomes the bearer of information for other subjects, which, through the intermediary of the object, then assembles their inventive and organizational capacities with those of the inventor.

As we have seen, that technical activity is the model of collective relation does not mean that the human would be essentially a prosthetic being; nor does it mean that there would only be collective individuation through technics: Simondon himself warns us against such a misinterpretation by specifying that technical activity "is not the only mode and the only contents of the collective, but it is of the collective, and, *in certain cases*, it is around technical activity that the collective group may be born" (*MEOT*, 245; emphasis added). In other words, even when transindividual relation between humans results from an adequate relationship to technical objects, because it conditions them in return, it can only *guarantee* such a relationship. Significantly, at the conclusion of his work on technics, Simondon insists that constitution of a transindividual mode of relation to technics is necessary for enabling us to apprehend technical objects in light of the sedimented preindividual within them. But this only makes sense if it is true that disalienated relation to technical objects, a use of machines adequate to the power of amplification of the contemporary technical network, can be opened within transindividual collective.

In Conclusion

Constructing a fair relationship to technics, which is the difficult objective that Simondon's thought establishes for our times, definitely does not mean rediscovering an always repressed originary: what technicity can do as an amplifying network is yet to be invented. If I have here rejected the reduction of Simondon to the image of a thinker of technics, it is not in order to keep technics on the order of a means for action. It is Simondon's virtue to have seen that technics *as network* now constitutes a milieu that conditions human action. Out of that milieu, we need simply to invent new forms of fidelity to the transductive nature of beings, both living and nonliving, with new transindividual modalities for amplifying action. For, in our relation to preindividual nature, multiple strands of relation—to others, to machines, to ourselves—entwine in a loose knot or node, and that is where thought and life come once again into play.

Afterword: Humans and Machines

Thomas LaMarre

While the wave of fascination with cyborgs, both in popular culture and cultural analysis, seems to have peaked and abated, the thorny question of the relation between humans and machines persists. In fact, the fascination with cyborgs seemed to reach an impasse, blocking rather than opening further inquiry. Ian Hacking notes something of the sort in his essay "Canguilhem amid the Cyborgs,"[1] suggesting a certain proximity between Descartes and Donna Haraway in their take on the relation between humans and machines. Hacking offers this passage from Haraway's celebrated "Cyborg Manifesto": "Late twentieth century machines have made thoroughly ambiguous the difference between natural and artificial . . . and many other distinctions that apply to organisms and machines."[2] If such wisdom about cyborgs reaches an impasse, it is because the emphasis ultimately falls on a blurring of distinctions. As such, it would seem that there is in fact an initial and fundamental distinction to be made between humans and machines, or between organisms and mechanisms, which subsequently becomes blurred and confused upon the appearance of the cyborg. Also, because the status of this human–machine distinction is not clear (is it a societal bias, cultural fantasy, false abstraction, or all of these?), it comes to feel like a substantialist distinction. Even as it proposes to blur distinctions, this sort of cyborg model unwittingly begins to take on the weight of dualism and substantialism, acting as if humans and machines were substantially different, and mobilizing a range of dualist oppositions (nature–artifice, mind–body, organic–inorganic) only to posit a subsequent fusing and blurring of them.

Put another way, this cyborg wisdom entails a simplistic hybridity model: identities have ontological priority, and the subsequent combination of two identities is experienced as a crisis of categories. Seen in this light, it becomes clear that the cyborg model implies a juridical model of power in which the distinction between humans and machines is a matter of law, a de jure distinction. This is why the cyborg or human–machine hybrid comes to be seen as a form of transgression or subversion. This is also why the cyborg model often appears ambivalent about, or even indifferent to, the de facto relations between humans and machines, that is, the actual techniques that couple human and machine, and the kinds of governance that simultaneously emerge to regulate them. What counts in the cyborg model is the blurring of the law, what renders law ambiguous or transgresses it. Because of this underlying reliance on a juridical conceptualization of power and thus on sovereignty, the cyborg model lingers not only on law and transgression but also on fantasies of disembodiment and intransivity, that is, on instances of unpredicated or self-predicating subjectivity, which, in keeping with the connotations of the prefix "cyber" as "guidance," "steering," or "navigation," prepare the way for the cybernaut as the new great helmsman.[3]

Simondon's thinking on humans and machines proceeds in a totally different manner.[4] Rather than blur or collapse the distinction between human and machine, or for that matter, organism and mechanism, he sustains it yet stubbornly refuses to allow it to take on substantialist weight. Thus, for him, humans and machines are different; they can even be said to be ontologically different, but within an ontology that methodologically avoids dualism and substantialism, which is indeed more precisely called *ontogenesis*. The same holds for bodies and minds: they are different, but not substantially, and likewise organisms and machines, as well as living beings and technical beings: different, but not in accordance with dualism or substantialism. In this respect, Simondon also parts ways with Heideggerian ontology as well as its deconstruction, for his ontogenetic perspective does not hinge on a distinction between beings and Being, or between the ontic and ontological. The Heideggerian lineage tends toward an unending (deconstructive) displacement of substantialism, rather than finding new points of departure. The cyborg model, as I have characterized it, oscillates between two understandings of technology: on the one hand, a Heideggerian or post-Heideggerian deconstructionist understanding that speaks of an "essence of technology" while ultimately resorting to a linguistic model for techniques, which tends to bring everything back under the signifier, law, and Being; and on the other hand, Norbert Wiener's cybernetic theory, which, for all his interest in and admiration for it, Simondon thought quite dangerous in its tendency to blur the distinction between animals and machines, ultimately reducing the human and society to one paradigm of the machine.

In contrast, Simondon's interest lies not in Law or Being (quasi-juridical distinctions between Being and beings, and an incessant blurring and reasserting of them), but in what he calls, and means quite literally, "modes of existence" of technical objects, that is, the ontology of machines. In a manner of speaking, then, an "essence of technology" emerges in Simondon's account of machines. But his account does not assume, on the one hand, a distinction between technique and technology, which invariably tends toward substantialism; rather, his use of the term "technics" (*la technique*) comprises both. As such, on the other hand, the "essence of technology" does not pose a metaphysical threat in the form of covering over Being with mere beings. If we wish to think in terms of a metaphysical threat, for Simondon it comes from dualism, substantialism, and hylomorphism—that is, operative ways of thinking and doing technology. While Heidegger's notion of "gaining a free relation to technology" might be construed as analogous to Simondon's move to think and do technics differently, Simondon does not fret endlessly over the conditions of (im)possibility for a different relation to technology. Perhaps because of his training in sciences and engineering, Simondon confidently speaks of an inherent value to technics, which he calls "technicity."

Owing to its focus on technics and technicity, Simondon's philosophy implies a very different conceptualization of power and of politics than the juridically orientated conceptualization of law and transgression implicit in the cyborg model. With the renewal of interest in Simondon in recent years, several commentators, among them Muriel Combes, Isabelle Stengers, Brian Massumi, Bruno Latour, and Alberto Toscano, have begun to explore some of those political implications, albeit going in rather different directions. This afterword has two goals. On the one hand, it aims to tease out some of the political implications of Simondon's philosophy of technics. Here, as my choice of terminology already indicates, I tend to see a dialogue between Simondon and Foucault as both suitable and productive. But, in the course of this essay, I also put Simondon in relation to Rancière (the notion of aesthetic equality) as well as Latour and Stengers (nonhuman actors and cosmopolitics). On the other hand, because the political implications of Simondon are grounded in his philosophy, this essay necessarily reviews or rehearses the central points of his ontogenetic perspective. Throughout my account, I am implicitly building on Muriel Combes's brilliant introduction to Simondon's philosophy, but with a focus primarily on the ontological distinction that he makes between physical beings, technical beings, and human beings. I consistently try to situate Simondon's approach in relation to the philosophy of history and science, in the hope of providing a complement to Combes's work and paying a compliment to it.

Physical Being

In *Du mode d'existence des objets techniques* (On the mode of existence of technical objects [*MEOT*], 1958), Simondon methodologically situates the role or function of the human *between* machines. For instance: "The human comprehends machines; he has a role to play between machines rather than over and above them, if there is to be a true technical ensemble" (*MEOT*, 138). Already in this brief passage, we find terms that merit attention. What is this "human comprehending" that implies that humans should situate themselves between machines and enable true (*véritable*) technical ensembles?

As a first step, we might note that, when Simondon says that humans' role or function is to be between machines, he means this biologically. Following his mentor Georges Canguilhem, whose thought he radicalizes, Simondon begins with a sort of inversion of the cybernetic perspective: instead of reducing organisms to machines, he opts to look at the operations of machines by analogy to the structures and functions of organisms.[5] Simondon's approach thus resonates with Canghuilhem's point of departure: "Tools and machines are kinds of organs, and organs are kinds of tools and machines."[6] Technology is neither in opposition to biology, nor over and above the human body, but a continuation of it. Nor is technology situated as lesser to or below science, as a mere application of it, that is, as a lesser set of procedures than the "higher" functions of the human mind. As Henning Schmidgen notes, "In Canguilhem's eyes, technology was more than a secondary result of scientific activity. To him it testified to some irreducible, biologically grounded mode of activity."[7] As such, when Simondon writes that the role of humans is between machines, his refusal to introduce a dualist divide between humans and machines extends to other registers, such as the relation between mind and body. Not only is there no substantialist opposition between mind and body, but also there are no hierarchical distinctions between levels of intellectual activity: technical activity is on par not only with biological function, but also with scientific thinking. Rather than fall back on dubious hierarchical rankings and teleological development (to wit, first comes the physical, then the vital, then the practical, and then the intellectual or logical, which sequence is construed as moving from the lower or lesser to the higher and superior), Simondon generates operative analogies across these gradations of complexity, using parity to get at disparity.

Such an approach might seem to verge on biological determinism, merely getting rid of questions about the mind, soul, or psyche by pinning everything on biological determinations, in the manner of sociobiology. But this is not at all the case. For all that Simondon draws heavily on biology in his philosophy of technology, he is equally fond of physics, which serves as another reminder that the rejection of dualism and substantialism in Simondon entails a shift from dialectics to *energetics*, as Alberto Toscano puts it.[8] In other words, his approach is not that of material determinism (whether that of genes or atoms, or certain manners of dialectical thinking). Instead, in keeping with the fact that neither genes nor atoms are foundational in contemporary sciences, Simondon's approach eschews material determinism, looking to what might be called "energetic determinations," or more precisely, in the language of physics that he adopts, *dephasings* or *phase shifts*. That Simondon occasionally glosses dephasing as "doubling" (*dédoubler*) indicates that he is not intent on dispensing with contrasts or conflicts. Rather, it is a matter of not beginning (and thus ending) with an ontological dualism, with a scission between spirit and substance (substantialism), between human and nature (dialectics), between human and machine (cybernetics), or between form and matter (hylomorphism).[9]

Yet Simondon's turn to energetics is not intended simply to dissolve those entities that appear concrete to us into a play of forces or field of energies. On the contrary, in attending to the underlying energetics of concrete entities in an abstract fashion, Simondon wishes to figure out what gives consistency to specific kinds of "individuals." Thus, when Simondon looks at an individual from the point of view of its individuation—that is, its dephasing, its underlying energetics—his goal is not to dissolve the concrete individual into abstract forces or to hold the individual under erasure. Instead he aims at a systematic account of how an individual can enter into relations with other individuals. In this respect, as Didier Debaise aptly stresses, Simondon's focus on the individual is calculated as a systematic intervention into modernity, into the modern condition of knowledge in which the individual has been given analytic priority in nearly every discipline, from the natural sciences to the human sciences.[10] And it is worth stressing that Simondon's exploration is systematic in that he sticks to the analytics of individuation across physics, chemistry, biology, engineering, psychology, sociology, and politics. In effect, he works through the knowledge of the individual that is generated within each of these disciplines, to arrive at a deeper and more systematic reading of that individual by giving analytic priority to its individuation, that is, to the process whereby it gains or has gained consistency or concreteness.

In another language, we might say that Simondon looks at the individual as an open system rather than a closed system. But then, for Simondon, it is not merely a matter of stressing the openness or nonfinished nature of the individual, but rather of exploring its specific kind of openness, that is, the implicit limits or potential orientations enabling such openness. In other words, the individual remains open in that its relations imply an underlying set of potentials, which at once grounds and exceeds the actual relations that it has established. If Simondon's philosophy is aptly characterized as a "philosophy of individuation" as well as a "philosophy of relations," it is because his focus on the individuation of the individuals in different domains necessarily entails giving real priority to the relation over the terms of the relation. Below, I will return to his emphasis on thinking the relation. But first, in keeping with the concreteness of Simondon's abstractions, let me look at one of his paradigms for thinking physical individuation—the formation of crystals, such as ice crystals from super-cooled water, or mineral crystals from a supersaturated aqueous solution.

The crystal is an instance of a form or structure. Focusing on the process of emergence of a form or structure, Simondon challenges received ways of thinking about form. In particular, he rejects the schema in which form is imposed upon matter, in which matter figures as a passive recipient for the active imposition of structure or form, for such a schema, also called hylomorphism, implies dualism and substantialism from the outset. With the example of crystallization, whether of ice from supercooled water or of minerals from a supersaturated solution, Simondon shows the inadequacy of the form–matter opposition for understanding actual processes. He shows that we cannot simply begin with the form or structure (crystal) as a self-identical, autonomous, given individual. Instead he demonstrates that the individual is always in process. The individual is individuating, dephasing, becoming. This does not simply mean that everything, no matter how stable in appearance, is actually in flux and thus ephemeral. Simondon reminds us that, if something appears stable to us, that stability is relative to a frame of reference, or more precisely, to a *concern*.[11] And that frame of reference appears stable because, as a concern, it is also individuating, that is, it is *operatively* producing a connection between different orders of magnitude. I will return to the notion of a concern below. But first let me continue with the stakes of individuation for Simondon.

In her presentation, Muriel Combes provides a fine description of the physical process of crystallization, highlighting the significance of metastability in Simondon's enlarged, energetic account of the individual:

> A physical system is said to be in metastable equilibrium (or false equilibrium) when the least modification of system parameters (pressure, temperature, etc.) suffices to break its equilibrium. Thus, in super-cooled water (i.e., water remaining liquid at a temperature below its freezing point), the least impurity with a structure isomorphic to that of ice plays the role of a seed for crystallization and suffices to turn the water to ice. Before all individuation, being can be understood as a system containing potential energy. Although this energy becomes active within the system, it is called potential because it requires a transformation of the system in order to be structured, that is, to be actualized in accordance with structures. Preindividual being, and in a general way, any system that is in a metastable state, harbors potentials that are incompatible because they belong to heterogeneous dimensions of being. This is why preindividual being can be perpetuated only by *dephasing*.

In referring us to metastability and dephasing instead of positing a form–matter distinction, Simondon moves beyond a dualist mode, introducing a series of parameters into his account of form, structure, or individual. There are, in effect, four parameters: (1) the seed or germ that sets off crystallization; (2) the supersaturated solution before crystallization; (3) the crystal; and (4) the less saturated aqueous solution after crystallization. Let's look more closely at these four parameters in order to clarify the abstract paradigm that Simondon extracts from this physical individuation.

First, the seed or germ that makes the crystalline structure materialize out of the supersaturated solution is, in a sense, just a tiny little impurity. But along the surface of that little impurity is a moment or site that is configured in a manner that is isomorphic to the coming crystal. For instance, if you ever made "rock candy" by crystallizing sugar on a string by dipping it into a supersaturated solution, you know that the string doesn't look at all like the resultant crystals that form on it. But somewhere along the string is a sort of isomorphic trigger that starts the crystallization. This trigger may be so small that we might never be able to identify or isolate it precisely. It is, then, in abstract terms, a point. And as Brian Massumi styles it, it is a "neutral point."[12] It is a point, *the* point, that starts the event of crystallization, but it is part of the event, not outside of it. It is physically inside the crystal, continuous with its structure, and at the same time, just as the string remains distinct from the crystals that form upon it, this neutral point is equally outside the crystal. Subsequently, when dealing with the history of technology, Simondon introduces the notion of an "absolute origin,"[13] which is like a neutral point. But there is a slight distinction. We can think of the neutral point in relation to the physical form of the crystal, as a given, while the absolute origin refers to the eventfulness that is triggered by the neutral point, the activation of the field of potential energy. The proximity of neutral point and absolute origin helps us to understand how this neutral point functions: the relations triggered or activated by the neutral point are relative, but the entire set of relations, potential and actual, are *relative to* an absolute origin (an eventfulness), which allows them to be operative as well as measurable within a frame of reference, or more precisely, within a concerned relation.

Let me force the analogy and say that the absolute origin is eventful like the speed of light within the general theory of relativity. There is a universe of general relativity, but relations are relative to the speed of light in that universe. Likewise, the event of crystallization entails the activation of an individuating "world" or "universe" whose relations are relative to an absolute origin. While I envision plenty of reasonable objections to my forced analogy, I like this analogy because it highlights in advance a basic question that is often posed of such an approach: if events of individuation set up relativistic worlds, how do worlds or universes interact? In other words, how will Simondon move beyond the problem of preestablished harmony that informed Leibniz's monadology?

Second, there is the supersaturated solution, which, Combes tells us, is an instance of metastable equilibrium. Alberto Toscano speaks of it as a "transcendental field populated by singularities and disparate series."[14] In other words, it is a transcendental field of disparation. In a sense, it is a disparity between orders of magnitude that is deeper than or prior to potentiality or potential energy itself. The neutral point, that little germ of germination, activates a field of potential energy, which is what Simondon calls preindividual being. An individual always implies a part or share of preindividual being, a field of potentiality.[15] But, if we tried to trace back from this field to the neutral point, the neutral point would always appear to be missing as a given point. It is rather like tracing back the movement of galaxies away from the big bang: although it seems that you might be able to trace movement back to a point, you arrive at something where space and time relations cannot be so nicely sorted out. In this respect, Simondon's disparation appears close to the Deleuzian notion of the plane of immanence or the plane of consistency. The relation between the neutral point and its "field" of preindividual being is rather like the relation between center and circumference in medieval definitions of God—"a circle whose center is everywhere, and whose circumference is nowhere," in that the center and circumference present two sides of the same event.

But then, Simondon's notion of disparation could not be drawn with a holistic geometric figure like a circle. In any event, Simondon constantly draws examples from concrete individuals, insisting that the abstraction is nothing without such a focus on, and concern for, concrete individuation (or in Whitehead's language, concrescence), and so his manner of thinking also puts disparation into practice, analogically, expressing it operatively in divergent series. There is no such thing as preestablished harmony (geometrical holism).

Third, there is form or structure, that is, the crystal or individuated being itself, which is precisely what Simondon aims to think in depth. As such, again following Massumi's turn of phrase, we can think of this form or structure in terms of "remarkable points." Needless to say, the term "remarkable" brings into play questions about apperception, perception, and comprehension, which returns us to Simondon's theory of analogy. Here too, lest his theory of analogy appear to offer too beautiful a solution, Debaise reminds us that we must think about this procedure of analogy precisely as a procedure or operation, or to use his terms, as technique or paradigm.[16] In other words, to call attention to remarkable points is not a neutral gesture but an analogically constructive cut or an operative fold in reality. In effect, the ground for Simondon's politics becomes clearer here: he refutes the realism that takes structure or form to be reality; instead he sticks to the realism of relation in order to show not only that the individual is in process but also that stopping or prolonging that process brings into play a *dispositif* (to use Foucault's term), that is, a set of techniques, an "apparatus" or "paradigm," around which procedures of territorialization, discipline, or control may gather.[17]

Fourth, there is the aqueous solution around the crystal, which we can initially gloss as an external milieu. Insofar as the crystal is a set of remarkable points, this external milieu is the ground (*fonds*) against which the remarkable points become precisely remarkable. In other words, Simondon sees the emergence of a duality with the emergence of an individuated being. This duality is not that of dialectical opposition but what might be called *contrast*. The relation between individual and external milieu is like that between form and ground, or figure and background. But this analogy will remain confined to an art historical paradigm unless we take another step with Simondon and consider how the milieu is not only external to form or structure but also internal to it. In the case of the crystal, we can think concretely of the water trapped within the crystalline lattice even after the crystal leaves its aqueous solution. But the internal milieu is not merely water left behind. It is a matter of *spacing*, and we might here think of spacing in a Foucauldian way, in terms of potentiality and power.

But this fourth parameter in Simondon's example of crystallization is neither the external milieu nor the internal milieu but the two of them taken together. It is the relation between external and internal milieu that matters, and Simondon often refers to it as an associated milieu. The associated milieu is what runs across the structure's contrast (external milieu) and spacing (internal milieu). It is thus the ground of the ground, the true ground, as it were. And, where terms such as "contrast" and "spacing" have largely spatial and static connotations, the associated milieu is energetic, charged, potentiality. If we continue with the example of the crystal, recall that, when you remove the crystal from its aqueous solution, it ceases to grow. Put it back in, and new layers of crystal form. This is because the internal milieu and external milieu are brought back into communication, rediscovering the preindividual share or field of potentiality, which allows the individuation to continue. In sum, the associated milieu is the energetically charged field running across internal spacing and external contrast.[18]

I have lingered on Simondon's account of the individuation of the crystal because all too often the example of the crystal is extended metaphorically without any deeper consideration of Simondon's analytics, and consequently, every instance of individuation comes to look exactly like that of the crystal, that is, physical being. This metaphoric evocation of the crystal runs the risk of erasing the very differences that matter to Simondon. Simondon does not simply extend his account of the physical being to natural or living being, technical being, and so forth, erasing their differences. Again, he establishes parity in order to account for disparity. He explores the underlying processes that generate individuals in terms of the four parameters presented above: (1) remarkable points, that is, form or structure of the individual; (2) the charged ground or potentialized associated milieu of the individual that is at once external contrast and internal spacing; (3) the neutral point of the event (absolute origin) of individuation that simultaneously sets off individuation and arises in it; and (4) the field of preindividual being, which is the specific activation associated with a specific neutral point, that is, the specific activation of a relation between disparate orders of magnitude that "potentializes" or "energizes" the process of individuation. In sum, to think other modes of existence analogically (not metaphorically) with the example of physical being, we need to look at the individual in terms of a sort of energized topological configuration that has remarkable points, a charged ground (contrast and spacing), a neutral point, and a plane of disparation crossing orders of magnitude.[19]

We should also keep in mind that, for Simondon, the individuals in question are not just out there, as forms or structures that preexist human thought. Rather, these individuals are also those given to us by modern sciences and disciplines: sociology approaches society as an individual; psychology takes up the psyche as its individual; biology sets up life forms, cells, or species, as individuals; media studies works through the isolation of different media; and so forth. For Simondon, the problem of modernity, then, is twofold. On the one hand, there are signs in Simondon of a Foucauldian concern for how knowledge constructs its objects, because the apparatuses or paradigms that discipline, regulate, normativize, or control specific individuals tend to generate knowledge precisely by erasing individuation (process) and treating the individual (structure or form) as given. Simondon's focus on individuation as process evokes the absolute origin of the form–ground relation in order to repotentialize the ground of the (modern) individual, because this is where resistance (in the electrical sense) to nonprogressive modes of rationalization is already at work, where resistance may be brought into play, activated, or potentialized in progressive ways.

On the other hand, unlike Foucault, who, despite his interest in Thomas Kuhn's paradigms as a manner of rethinking history, shied away from the so-called normal sciences,[20] Simondon turns to individuation as process in order to address what he sees as another dangerous tendency of modern knowledge: the isolation of disciplines from one another on the basis of their construction of different individuals (society, psyche, medium, organism, species, machine) that are not allowed to communicate with one another, whose relationality becomes unthinkable. And he dislikes two common responses to this situation: the large metaphysical erasure of difference (every discipline is really talking about the same thing), and what I have somewhat unfairly characterized as the cyborg model, that is, a remix or mash-up of individuals from different domains without any concern for relationality, for actual differences, techniques, apparatuses, and paradigms. This is why Simondon works so intently within and across different domains of knowledge: he aims for a truly concerned multidisciplinarity. Placing the human between machines is one of the major concerns for moving in that direction. In this respect, if we wish to retain terms and phenomena such as "remix" or "cyborg," for instance, Simondon offers a way to engage them at a deeper level than a frenetic yet indifferent disassembly and reassembly of received, socially sanctified individuals.

Technical Being

Simondon replaces the distinction between organism and mechanism with a distinction between natural object and technical object, surely because the former terms have been inextricably entwined with dualist thought to the point where they tend to imply a substantialist distinction between nature and artifice, nature and culture, or nature and humans. And so, in styling both organisms and mechanisms as "objects," he reminds us that these beings or modes of existence are ontologically different in degree (analogous), not ontologically different in kind or nature (substantially). Still, to style organisms as "natural objects" may strike some readers as highly objectifying, in a manner reminiscent of positivism.[21] The term "object" for Simondon does not, however, imply objectification. In fact, although the scope of this essay doesn't permit a full treatment of the issue, suffice it to say, in keeping with his general refusal to posit substantialist divides, that Simondon sees subject and object as two sides of the same coin. Or rather, since the coin metaphor introduces too much symmetry into subject–object relations, we would do better to say that subject and object are different points of view across the same reality, that is, on the same relation.[22]

In the modern tendency toward the construction of technical individuals (machines), Simondon sees the emergence of a new kind of relation in which technical objects become more and more like natural objects—in that they carry their associated milieu with them, generating it through their relations. It is as if the crystal had folded its aqueous solution inside it, and could continue to grow or individuate by stoking its potentiality. Indeed, as Combes points out, Simondon does not see the passage from one mode of existence to another—say, from physical being to natural or vital being—in terms of a linear advance. Rather, developments that appear to come after or to be added to prior stages actually entail a return to what is ontologically prior, through a reimmersion in the preindividual. Just as an animal starts as an inchoate plant, so a natural individual begins as an inchoate physical individual. It is a general problem of modern thought that a substantial difference between life (natural object) and nonlife (physical object) is presumed as a point of departure. And it is a tendency that becomes particularly pronounced and reified in the context of the natural object versus the technical object. Countering this tendency, we may say that the technical individual is initially an inchoate human individual, but then we would have to add that its inchoate beginning or return to preindividual is analogous, not identical, to the inchoate start of the animal in the plant, for instance.

Consequently, although one of Simondon's key points is that, under conditions of modernity, technical individuals are becoming closer to natural individuals, he does not blur the ontological distinction between them. Indeed, Simondon's comments on popular attitudes toward robots and automatons, in which machines become so like humans that they begin to replace them, are pointedly deflationary ("We would like precisely to show that the robot does not exist," *MEOT*, 10), to the point where I don't think it an exaggeration to say that he sees in the tendency to collapse or conflate distinctions between natural objects and technical objects, not merely a metaphysical error but a form of moral panic as well, which ultimately serves to depoliticize the technical existence of humans. Near the end of the first part of *Du mode d'existence des objets techniques*, he strives to clarify the stakes historically and politically: as, in modern times, humans have constructed machines that can bear tools and thus replace them as technical individuals or tool bearers, humans have tended wrongly to apply ideas of slavery and freedom to this new relation (*MEOT*, 82). Such a mistake is not purely or simply psychological in origin. It derives from actual conditions in which humans now tend to work over or under machines, rather than alongside them. Yet, when humans look at their relationship to machines in terms of slavery and freedom, they merely repeat these conditions, striving either to liberate themselves from machines or to enslave the machines once and for all. Needless to say, the fear of a robot revolution grows as a result. Simondon's comments suggest that thinking in (largely juridical) terms of human freedom from, or mastery over, machines constitutes a genuine blockage for progressive politics. This is why he pointedly remarks, "The robot does not exist" (*MEOT*, 10). This is also why I began by contesting the cyborg model in which a fascination with the blurring of the distinction between humans and machines, oscillating breathlessly between technophilia and technophobia, forecloses any reckoning with technical equality or technicity and reifies the paradigm of freedom and slavery by displacing it onto juridical paradigms of law and transgression.

If Simondon singles out this wrong thinking about freedom for attention, it is not because his politics bear no relation to democracy or freedom. On the contrary, when he insists on the ontological equality between humans and machines, he is positing something analogous to what Rancière styles as "aesthetic equality." For Rancière, aesthetic equality, as it emerges in modern art and literature, is not the same thing as political equality, but by emphasizing how aesthetic equality may ground, condition, and even spur democracy, Rancière definitively shifts the site of the political away from an exclusive focus on the rational and juridical (and by extension, the sovereign State).[23] Aesthetic equality, then, is a matter of equal participation in aesthetic production, which does not preclude difference; indeed, it assumes it. Similarly, when Simondon insists on ontological equality between humans and machines, he implies a sort of "technical equality," which is another way of describing "technicity." As with Rancière's notion of aesthetic equality, technicity implies equal technical participation even as it presumes difference. While technical equality, like aesthetic equality, is no guarantee of political equality or democracy, political equality is not practical or operative without a relation to this technical operativity (which is also, like aesthetics, a sort of inoperativity in the sense that it refuses utilitarian operativity).

How, then, does Simondon strive to bring technicity into the modern relation between humans and machines? His discussion advances on two fronts, the one ontological, the other historical. Thus he speaks in terms of the essence of technical objects at the same time that he speaks of a modern historical transformation that brought the technical individual to the fore. Of course, insofar as the hallmark of Simondon's thought lies in its emphasis on *ontogenesis* (becoming) rather than ontology (being), it may be more appropriate to say that his argument addresses the *ontogeny* and *phylogeny* of technical individuals, for, on the one hand, he considers what a technical individual is as a mode of existence (ontogeny), and on the other hand, he explores the natural history or evolution of its "group" (phylogeny).[24]

To approach these points, let me turn to how Simondon's account of the ontogenesis of the technical individual can be understood by analogy with the abstract schema outlined above in the context of the physical individual, the crystal. Technical individuation, like individuation in general, can be seen in terms of the emergence of a specific configuration of remarkable points, that is, a specific form or structure. In the case of technical individuation, Simondon calls attention to a passage from the abstract to the concrete, which he styles as *concrétude*, that is, concrescence or concretization. As we will see, however, such concretization is not a matter of making form or structure (the determinate) more concrete. Rather, it is the indeterminate that takes on concreteness; concrescence lies in the solidarity of openness.

When he looks at the individuation of machines from the angle of the process of invention, Simondon sees a passage from an abstract, analytical, logical system toward a concrete, synthetic, practical system. Inventors begin designing machines with an eye to accomplishing a single task, which they diagram in an abstract, analytic fashion; but as they actually use the machine, the design itself begins to demand practical adjustments, bringing into play other aspects of its basic elements, adding new elements, and creating new relations among elements. For instance, you design a motor to turn a wheel without necessarily thinking about the materials, but when building and operating it, you discover that certain materials, forged in a such as way as to produce specific qualities, work better. In effect, it becomes self-regulating. Usually it is a matter of a combination or synthesis of different materials, which is why Simondon sees a passage toward a concrete and synthetic system.

Still, if we remain at this level of analysis, we are considering only structure, not process, that is, individuation itself. And so Simondon introduces a twist: this passage toward concreteness is also a passage toward openness, toward greater indeterminacy. Where we might expect the perfected machine to be more closed, Simondon shows us that, in fact, the abstract logical diagram is more closed, while concrescence is a passage toward a more open system. We will not see this openness, however, if we attend only to the form and not to its ground or associated milieu. The associated milieu of the technical individual, like that of the physical individual (crystal), runs across the external milieu and internal milieu, grounding the structure of remarkable points. It is both spacing and contrast, or more precisely, charged spacing and charged contrast. And the charge or potential effectively runs through or across inside and outside, as a *transductive potential*. But let's turn first, as Simondon does, to the internal milieu of the technical individual.

Simondon characterizes the internal milieu of the machine in terms of *recurrent causality*. A host of other, apparently synonymous terms also peppers his account, such as "circular causality," "circularity," "recursive causality," "reciprocal relations," and even "feedback loop." "Recurrent causality" is by far the favored expression. But what does this term mean? As the technical individual becomes more concrete, synthetic, and practical, its internal ground, the spacing between elements, ceases to be empty space; it ceases to rely on purely logical relations. The inventor begins to see that elements can be used with more than one function, for instance, thus tightening up the relations between elements as well as producing the possibility for internal circularity, feedback, reciprocity, or recurrence, and thus, ultimately, for self-regulation. I should add that, although I am presenting this transformation from the point of view of the inventor, it is clear that the invention, on its side, can be said to enable and suggest such concretization. It is not passively altered. Technical individuation proposes connections and new relations. Although it is too much to say that the machine is thinking for itself, it is clear that the inventor and invention are thinking with one another, and this thinking, insofar as it is a relation, is on both sides, and it is entirely real.

As a glance at the images in *Du mode d'existence* attests, one of the virtues of Simondon's account is its wealth of detailed examples, from audiometers to car engines to cathode tubes, which he works through as he systemically qualifies his argument about what counts as a technical individual.[25] Some machines are ruled out (the audiometer); others are tentatively included but only with qualification. For my purposes here, a very basic example will suffice. When Simondon addresses the cooling of the automobile engine, he weighs the merits of air-cooling and water-cooling (*MEOT*, 25). Air-cooled engines are more concrete, because you don't have to add a subsystem to the engine: the air element is directly there. Water-cooling is semiconcrete. If you could produce water from the running of the engine and redirect it for cooling, or if you could power the water circulation directly from the engine, the engine would become more concrete. In practice, however, water is circulated via a water pump driven by a separate drive belt. Nonetheless, Simondon concludes that water-cooling is more concrete than air-cooling if you look at the engine in terms of security measures, for water absorbs and disperses heat more effectively than air. In other words, insofar as introducing water allows for better self-regulation, it encourages concretization, but water is not part of the immediate operating environment of the engine as air is.

Simondon's discussion here is not conclusive, and that is precisely why it offers a fine sense of the practical technical considerations that arise between human and machine in the course of concrescence. Its inconclusiveness also serves as a reminder that this manner of thinking technicity is resistant to finality or teleology (which Simondon also calls "hypertelia"). Although one may detect echoes of Aristotelian entelechy in Simondon's take on the machine, because Simondon goes beyond form into its underlying and surrounding processes, the finality associated with entelechy gives way to relationality, here in the mode of technicality. As such, technicality does not proceed in a linear, continuous fashion. Simondon sums it up thus:

> Thus it would not suffice to say that the technical object is one whose specific genesis proceeds from the abstract to the concrete; it should be made clear that this genesis is achieved by essential, discontinuous improvements that make for the internal schema being modified in leaps and bounds and not according to a continuous line. (*MEOT*, 40)

Simondon turns next to the external milieu of technical individuation. Recall that, in the example of crystallization, a dephasing or an onset of form simultaneously produced a surrounding milieu, which is less structured but nonetheless charged with potential. In the case of the machine, similarly, the phase shift producing it also implies the simultaneous appearance of an external milieu. Significantly, the external milieu of the machine, like its "internal ground," entails a "recurrence of causality" (*MEOT*, 57). Here too, Simondon offers a range of examples of the reciprocal or recurrent relations of causality that arise between the technical object and its external milieu, but as with the crystal, what is crucial is the associated milieu that both links and grounds this link between internal and external milieus. With the machine, its practical operations not only tend to associate it with a particular environment but also work actively to construct such an environment, as the machine works operatively on the field of potentiality grounding two sites of recurrent causality. In this way, the operations of the machine construct a mixed environment that is at once geographical and technical, which Simondon dubs a "technogeographical milieu." He also distinguishes this construction of an associated milieu from the humanization of nature. In other words, the new associated milieu is not an imposition of human will upon the environment but presents an opportunity for working with or alongside specific machine-environments or even machine ecologies. Simondon's discussion anticipates his account of "technical ensembles," which entail specific assemblages of humans, technical individuals or machines, technical elements, resources, and milieus, to which I will return.

First, however, because Simondon's vocabulary is naturalistic, I should point out that Simondon's aim is not to endorse any kind of relation between technical individuals and the environment, or to deny the widespread environmental destruction associated with modern technology. Rather, in a manner reminiscent of Heidegger's critique of merely technological behavior, Simondon sees the question of technology not in terms of an acceptance or rejection of technology to be articulated entirely in anthropocentric terms (human loss or gain), but in terms of establishing a different relation to technology, one that is implicit in technicity itself but that is currently disabled owing to what might be called metaphysical thinking.[26] In contrast with Heidegger, however, who gestured in this direction only to retreat, Simondon possesses greater technical and scientific know-how and proceeds with greater confidence and concern for actual sociohistorical hierarchies of technics, which leads to greater emphasis on actual human–machine relations and technosocial formations (that is, technical ensembles). In this respect, Simondon's account of machines bears comparison with the "nonhuman actors" that play a central role in the technopolitical theories of both Isabelle Stengers and Bruno Latour.

Both Stengers and Latour describe their approach as constructivist and cosmopolitical because it deals with the construction of new nonhuman actors whose actions demand new kinds of political response. Steven Shaviro summarizes their point of departure succinctly: "For modern science, the constructivist question is to determine how this practice is able (unlike most other human practices at least) to produce objects that have lives of their own, as it were, so that they remain 'answerable' for their actions in the world independently of the laboratory conditions under which they were initially elucidated. This is what makes neutrinos and microbes, for instance, different from codes of justice, or from money, or from ancestral spirits that may be haunting someone."[27] In other words, Stengers and Latour call attention to the modern scientific construction of specific nonhuman entities that begin to act in the world beyond the laboratory, in a manner reminiscent of Simondon's machines, even though, from the angle of Simondon's project, we might wish to characterize them as "scientific individuals" or "experimental individuals."

While both Stengers and Latour strategically pose some degree of equality or symmetry between human actors and nonhuman actors, they differ in that, generally speaking, the politics of "speaking with" nonhumans ultimately turns into a matter of *speaking for* nonhuman actors (that is, representation) for Latour, whereas in Stengers the emphasis falls on how we are *speaking about* nonhumans, that is, how to gauge the truth-claiming capabilities of the sciences. In her account of Whitehead's *Process and Reality*, for instance, she writes of "the need to actively and explicitly relate any knowledge-production to the question that it tries to answer" rather than to take it as a neutral statement or "conception of the world."[28]

Previously, with a nod to Rancière's notion of aesthetic equality, I have suggested the term "technical equality" to refer to Simondon's gesture of taking the equality of human and technical objects as a point of departure. And this is where Simondon's account of technical individuals intersects with Latour's and Stengers's interest in nonhuman actors. Yet Simondon also adds something crucial to the politics of technical equality. There is, of course, a difference in concern, insofar as Stengers's and Latour's focus might be best qualified as "experimental individuals" in contrast to Simondon's technical individuals. Yet, above and beyond this difference of focus, with his close attention to both the remarkable points (form) and associated milieu (across internal and external grounds) of the technical individual, Simondon's account introduces greater coherence at the level of what matters and how. What is more, because Simondon insistently specifies and qualifies what counts as a technical individual, his account shows greater concern for speaking with machines (or with technicity) rather than speaking for them (Latour's emphasis on representation) or about them (Stengers's focus on science's politics of truth). Finally, despite the generality of his historical account of modernity, Simondon offers a less massive theory of modernity than Latour in particular. In keeping with his focus on concrete specification, the technical individual for Simondon is one type or tendency within technical being, albeit one that becomes pronounced in modern times, whose dominance signals a kind of modernity. As such, his account invites us to think modernity in the manner of Foucault, not as a massive, all-encompassing rationalization or modernization, but in terms of overlapping fields of rationality (multiple modernities) with their specific potential for resistance.[29] This is because Simondon's attention to the associated milieu of the technical individual, in conjunction with its neutral point and remarkable points, brings technicity or technical equality into play with greater specification of potentiality.

To summarize the account of technical individuation thus far, what characterizes it is, first of all, the relation between form and ground. As the individual becomes concrete, it also differentiates, resulting in a stronger bifurcation of its ground into internal and external milieus. The ground of the crystal bifurcates into contrast and spacing, but, because these two aspects of the ground do not entail recurrent causality, they are not potentialized to the same degree that the doubling of the ground in technical individuation is. The ground of technical individual shows recurrent causality, both internally and externally. But these two sites of recurrent causality are not symmetrical or identical. As such, the internal ground and external ground have to "communicate" more actively across their asymmetry, and have to stabilize that communication. The result is a self-regulating individual, closer to a natural object than a physical object. But how are we to relate to this self-regulating individual?

It is here that Simondon's resistance to automatism is telling. He is as impatient with those who characterize machines in terms of automatism as he is with those who simply reject machines. Evidently, then, his emphasis on self-regulation is not an invitation for us to stand back and let machines run on their own, automatically. Rather, he continually reminds us, we're already involved in machines. There is something of the human in machines. At one level, this is obvious, since humans make machines. But, again for Simondon, it is not merely a matter of the human origins of machines in the sense that humans made machines and therefore can choose to use them or not to use them, for posing the question in this way leads us back to applying the paradigm of freedom versus slavery to human–machine relations. In other words, what is human in machines cannot be seized consciously or rationally in the sense of pure reason or cognition. In effect, how machines are "used" (or rather, participated in) should follow from how machines are invented. It is precisely because invention proceeds in a hands-on, practical, and inventive fashion, as a sort of dialogue between humans and machines that engages the preindividual within humans, that humans should not strive to "use" machines in a purely rational, utilitarian fashion. Rather, that relation to machines needs to sustain a practical inventive engagement with what is human in machines—in a word, technicity.

As Combes notes, such a view of human–machine relations is not compatible with a notion of technics as a means of compensating for or supplementing an originary lack, as Bernard Stiegler would have it. Stiegler seems to adopt a rather Lacanian point of departure: humans are deficient from birth; they are born too early, and to meet their needs, must compensate for their weakness, which they accomplish first by making tools and then machines. But, the argument goes, such compensation or supplementation goes far beyond needs, taking on a life of its own, so to speak. Thus machines swarm over the world, as a massive overcompensation for our weakness. Ultimately, then, the problem of human–machine relations turns into a psychoanalytic problem: only by recognizing and coming to terms with our primordial fragility will we be able to break our vicious cycles of technological overcompensation. Again, as Combes notes, such an understanding of technics, exemplified in Stiegler's notion of "originary technicity," is completely at odds with Simondon's understanding of technicity. It is not that Simondon does not countenance the fragility (or, we might say, precarity) of humans, but it is not for him an ontological ground. Humans for him are not originally or primarily fragile or lacking; they are also potentiality, capacity, powers in the world. Our situation vis-à-vis technics today is indeed precarious, but Simondon does not see it as a psychological or existential problem: if the situation is grim, it is not because we have ignored that we are ontologically constituted by lack. Rather, he says, we are practically alienated from our potentiality. As such, modern alienation is not ontologically given and thus predestined (deriving from lack) as in Stiegler. Instead, modern alienation is ontologically produced and historically constructed.

This is why the politics of Simondon's philosophy of individuation shows more affinity with Foucault and Rancière, despite the significant differences between their approaches: Simondon's approach is concerned with both the politics of knowledge and the politics of equality. On the one hand, like Foucault, Simondon sees knowledge as operative, as inseparable from power, and in this respect his critique of substantialism and hylomorphism, for instance, is not intended as a purely logical intervention, and his insistence on analogy is, in fact, an attempt to provide a knowledge whose operativity is adequate to the resistance implicated within the activation of fields around technical individuals. Here, however, we have to consider Simondon's distinction between three degrees of technical being: technical elements, technical individuals, and technical ensembles. The technical ensemble might be considered as analogous to Foucault's notion of a power/knowledge formation entailing a field of rationalization articulated upon a *dispositif,* a paradigm or apparatus. In such terms, the problem of modernity for Simondon is that the technical individual has been treated as the paradigm for a field of rationality, for the production of a specific kind of technical ensemble. Which is to say, the machine has been both practically seized and operatively rationalized into an automaton, which has generated technical ensembles (fields of rationality or power/knowledge) in which humans cannot work with technical individuals but only over them or below them (exemplified by but not limited to the factory, especially the Fordist assembly line).

On the other hand, in a manner closer to Rancière, Simondon is interested in equality, and in a specific mode of technical equality called technicity. Resistance to excessive rationalization of this specific field of rationality (say, the factory) would necessarily pass through such technical equality. And Simondon does not hesitate to say that technicity is inherently equalizing, that it makes for participation, which, like Rancière's aesthetic equality, may not guarantee political equality or democracy but surely conditions it. It is technicity that makes technical individuals the most important site for neutralizing and countering the subordination of all fields of rationality to economic concerns in the modern era.

In her account of Simondon, Combes astutely identifies the politics of labor as a point of intersection between these two ethico-political trajectories in Simondon's philosophy. Drawing on Antonio Negri and postoperaism in a truly prescient manner, Combes also shows how Simondon's account provides a rich source of counterknowledge for the post-Fordist era of information society in which knowledge has been built back into labor and production, making explicit that a factory was never just a production formation but always also a power/knowledge formation. Of course, for postoperaism, it is primarily the knowledge of workers that becomes the source of counterknowledge within the formation, and pursuing this line of inquiry, Combes suggests that one political complement to Simondon's project would be to take seriously what workers actually do with machines, and what they say about them, rather than dismiss them as servile and thus tending toward technophobia.

I am entirely in agreement with Combes on this point, and by way of conclusion, would like to open some possibilities for extending it to other kinds of counterknowledge/power that may effectively complement that of factory workers on machines. But to do so, I need to complete this account of the four aspects of individuation in the technical individual by considering its neutral point and absolute origin. In effect, the neutral point of the technical individual is the human, whose absolute origin or eventfulness is technicity. Here we come face to face with Simondon's humanism, that is, the centrality of the human being in his philosophy. Yet, as implied by terms such as absolute origin and neutral point, this human being is not that of traditional humanism, which is articulated juridically in terms of natural rights, natural sovereignty, or natural equality. Simondon's theory of human being hinges on the eventfulness of technicity.

Human Being

To look at a mode of existence in terms of its individuation is to look at it from the angle of the underlying and surrounding processes that are part of its genesis, making it what it is. The study of individuation recalls the study of evolution in this respect, for it is the study of the birth and transformation of individuals. As such, the individual is always in a series, and its ontogenesis is equally a phylogenesis, demanding a study of genesis (that is, a genealogy) from the angle of the series. Any inquiry into the relation between humans and machines, then, has to deal with a genealogy of the human alongside a genealogy of the technical object. Let's first look at the contours of genealogy in context of the technical object.

As I have explained above, the technical individual is a particular kind of technical object (a specific mode of technical existence). In the course of its individuation (concrescence), the technical individual generates zones of recurrent causality, both internally and externally, which are the charged transversal ground (associated milieu) for its efficient structuration of remarkable points. For Simondon, such developments bring the technical object closer to the natural object. The natural object also entails both an internal energetic "recurrent causality" between its elements and an external energetic "recurrent causality" with its surroundings that constructs an associated milieu.[30] In his account of the technical individual approaching the natural object, Simondon not only begins with the internal causality of the machine but also repeatedly defends this point of departure. Why is so much at stake in beginning with what happens *within* the technical individual, when we know that ultimately the associated milieu is what runs across and grounds external and internal milieus?

In ontogenetic terms, focusing on internal recurrent causality serves to highlight how the technical individual comes closer and closer to the natural object (but, of course, remains distinct ontologically nonetheless). But there is more at stake in Simondon's emphasis on the internal milieu. In genealogical or phylogenetic terms, his insistence on starting with what happens inside the machine is consistent with his rejection of the evolutionary model that is frequently called "adaptationism." Here, I would like to situate Simondon's theory of evolution alongside that of biologists and historians of science who have also challenged adaptationism, notably Stephen Jay Gould and Richard Lewontin, but also a range of other scientists and commentators who have explored the evidence against adaptationism and looked for alternative models for evolution.[31]

Critics of adaptationism argue that such an approach places too much emphasis on environmental pressures on the one hand, which leads, on the other hand, to the notion that, over time, as environments change, organisms are stuck with the adaptations produced by prior environments. This has contributed to the greatly exaggerated idea that contemporary humans are at a loss in the modern world because they were, in effect, evolved, that is, "hardwired" to deal with a very different environment. Adaptationism favors an account of external factors affecting evolutionary changes, largely ignoring the internal factors (both material limits and contingent opportunities, not to mention, what we might call in a Spinozan way, the powers of the body), which in turn encourages a very static, linear view of evolution. When Simondon refers to the emergence of recurrent causality within the machine as "internal adaptation," what is at stake for him is a model of evolutionary transformation that avoids the pitfalls of adaptationism (that is, "external adaptation" or adaptation from without). The focus on internal adaptations allows Simondon to avoid the model of a machine statically adapted to an environment, which then finds itself stranded and at a loss when the environment changes. Instead, like the natural object (organism), the technical individual effects internal changes and simultaneously generates a recurrent rapport with its external milieu, which allows it to interact actively with the world and to produce a transformative series. Again, this view of the technical individual is reminiscent of the nonhuman actor in Latour and Stengers, but to put it in a quasi-Spinozan way, Simondon is interested in the details of how specific technical bodies have the power to affect and to be affected.[32]

There is another concern in Simondon's emphasis on internal adaptation (which we might now also gloss as a sort of material involuntarism): he also wishes to complicate the relation between technical concerns and economic concerns. In the context of the evolution of technical individuals, Simondon's account implies an analogy between external factors and economic concerns. Thus the overemphasis on external factors within adaptationist theories of biological development is analogous to economic determinism in the context of technical development. In effect, implicit in his analogy between the focus on external factors in sociobiological determinism (adaptationism) and in economic determinism (economism) is a prescient critique of economism as a retooling of social Darwinism in the form economic Darwinism. While Simondon does not deny that there are times and places where economic concerns do indeed determine the direction of technical developments, he wishes to show the severe limitations of thinking technical evolution exclusively in terms of a subordination of the technical to the economic. In contrast, by insisting on the "equality" of the technical vis-à-vis the economic, Simondon finds a way to explore the relation—the fraught and tense relation—between the technical and economic.

As a corollary to his emphasis on the relative equality of the technical, Simondon also feels that an understanding of technical individuals based primarily on industry and factories is highly biased and overly narrow. Simondon thus encourages us also to consider dry docks, mines, oilfields, workshops, and laboratories. And in keeping with his strategy of analogy, Simondon encourages us to think the technical individual beyond the factory not merely because it is an error to remain focused on the factory, but because limiting our scholarly inquiry to an account of the factory reinforces the *dispositifs* that have operatively mistaken the machine for an automation and extended that operativity into fields of rationality and technical ensembles like the assembly line. For Simondon, the modern factory is a particularly noxious paradigm, which he posits as the prime site of alienation of the technicity of the human being. Combes is persuasive in pointing out that workers' knowledge of machines may not be simply alienated but may entail a complex alienation that includes possibilities for counterknowledge and transformation. And, to extend her insight operatively, we can also look into Simondon's genealogy of the human for other sites of complex gradations and counterknowledge/power.

Simondon's genealogy initially establishes that, with the modern emergence of true technical individuals or machines, humans find their previous role as technical individual taken from them. Which is to say, prior to modern machines, humans were the tool-bearers, playing the role of technical individuals. With the advent of technical individuals that bear tools, humans find themselves situated either below or above the machine. They become either caretakers of the machine or supervisors of ensembles of machines, a contrast reminiscent of that between worker and foreman or capitalist in Marx. For Simondon, such a genealogy is also remarkably close to the cyborg or cybernetic understanding of technicity, in which humans oscillate between enslaving machines and being enslaved by them. Not surprisingly, then, Simondon introduces a strange twist in this initially straightforward history: in fact, the role of tool-bearer, or of technical individual, does not rightly belong to humans. It is as if they had preemptively seized it from machines but had forgotten and come to mistake toolbearing as their function. In other words, while Simondon proposes a break with the industrial factory system that effectively makes humans into workers under, or supervisors over, machines, he is not interested in a return to a premodern guild or artisan formation in which the role of humans was closer to the technical individual. In effect, he is proposing that humans dig deeper into their evolutionary sources, to seek something prior to the technical being and human being that traverses them.

To understand this genealogical twist in which Simondon begins to dig deeper into both human being and technical being, we need to bear in mind that Simondon is working against adaptationism and its linear tendencies. Gould provides a good point of reference, for, in his major work, *Ontogeny and Phylogeny*, as he contests the emphasis on external environmental factors and digs deeper into the organism, his account arrives at an evolutionary theory based on heterochrony and neoteny.[33] Heterochrony is best illustrated in Gould's theory of punctuated equilibrium, in which evolution happens in bursts followed by long periods without transformation. Neoteny refers to the retention in adults of traits previously seen only in juveniles, which allows a species to undergo transformation from within, as it were. Examples of neoteny include the resemblance of dogs to immature wolves, flightless birds who resemble the chicks of flighted birds, and the large head and sparse body hair of humans, which recall baby primates. Neoteny might be thought of as a special case of heterochrony in that forward progress does not happen in a linear fashion but arises through a sort of return to the sources of being, a return to the point of bifurcation where potential energy is being converted into actual energy. Indeed, Simondon sees the relation between physical being and natural being in a similar fashion: the natural object does not simply advance from the physical object; rather the natural object presents a return to the point where potentiality is actualized, extending, internalizing, actualizing that potentialization. Figuratively speaking, the natural object is on the neotenous threshold of the physical object.

My point here is not that Simondon endorses neoteny as such, or that we should endorse neoteny. In fact, the term neoteny begins to mislead us if we think about it in terms of a literal movement backward in linear time. Rather, neoteny is one way to grasp concretely the role of pluripotentiality or preindividual being in the context of evolutionary development. As such, my evocation of neoteny is intended to shed light on some of the alternative ways of thinking ontogeny and phylogeny that come to the fore when the relentless linear pressure of adaptationism or economism is not accepted. Similarly to Gould, in his alternative nonadaptationist evolutionary theory of the evolution of humans and machines, Simondon will discover the heterochrony of technical evolution, which goes hand in hand with a mode of human being in relation to machines that is akin to neoteny. Looking at these aspects of Simondon's account will bring us to a better understanding of what it means for him to situate human being as the neutral point of the technical individual, with technicity as the absolute origin or eventfulness of technicity. Let's turn first to the heterochrony of technical phylogenesis.

Simondon sees the emergence of technical individuals or machines in modern times: with the gradual "liberation" of technical procedures that were formerly "enslaved" or inferiorized, that is, forcibly associated with lesser social positions and actively disavowed, inventors begin to attend to the potentiality within the operations of technical objects, resulting in machines. But Simondon is adamant: such progress is not a matter of greater automation but of a great margin of indetermination (due to recurrent causality) within machines and between machines and the world. This is technical individuation from the point of view of ontogeny, of the genesis of an individual machine, so to speak. But, because machines also exist in series and in ensembles, we also need to look at their phylogeny, at the relation between reproduction and transformation. On the basis of his running analogy with the natural object, Simondon notes that technical evolution is very different from that of organisms: with machines, it is as if the organ separated from the body and functioned as a seed or germ for a new individual or a new line of individuals. Thus we return to the point of the departure of this essay as well, to Canguilhem's analogy between machine and organism in which machines have organs like organisms. In Simondon, a similar analogy comes into play, which thoroughly defamiliarizes our sense of how machines form series.

For Simondon, the "organs" of the technical individual are its technical elements—its springs, blades, needles, and pulleys, to give a few examples. He refers to such technical elements as highly concretized forces or capacities, which is different from the concretization of technical individuals. It is as if the technical element had so thoroughly stabilized and concretized the recurrent causality of the machine that it approaches the limit of realizing its associated milieu. Technical elements can be used in a variety of milieus and thus made to work together in various kinds of technical individuals and technical ensembles. As forces for undergoing capacities or producing capacities, these technical elements might be said to be instances of technicity as such. Indeed, they bear a technical value independent of economic value. Because technical elements are autonomous, it is they who are transmitted to posterity—not the technical individual. In addition, because it is "organs" that are transmitted, the evolution of technical individuals implies a "line of causality that is not rectilinear but like the teeth of a saw, with the same reality existing in the form of an element, and then as a characteristic of the individual, and finally as a characteristic of the ensemble" (*MEOT*, 66).

In sum, technical being unfolds or evolves in series by articulating relations between three phases of its being, which are called technical elements, technical individuals, and technical ensembles. (Recall that the technical ensemble is like a field of rationality in which the technical individual is a mediator, a threshold for a paradigm or *dispositif*.) If Simondon describes the series of technical evolution as serrated, it is because he looks for resistance to the linear vision of technological progress in which we move from, say, the needle to the sewing machine, to the sweat shop that mobilizes scores of workers busy at their machines under the supervision of a boss, or to the fantasy of a completely automated garment factory without human workers at all. It is precisely this linear vision of technology that leads humans to fear the machine, for even the sewing machine implies a teleological movement toward the enslavement or ultimate redundancy of humans in the domain of fabrication. Simondon shows that there is no evidence that this is how things have proceeded or will proceed. Again, we suspect that if things have often turned out badly, it is because of the imposition of economic concerns upon technical individuation, which forces a rectilinear movement and a simplistic temporality of progress. In any event, Simondon's attention to the relation between three modes of technical being—element, individual, and ensemble—allows him to parse the heterochrony of technical evolution: technical evolution does not proceed from element (organ) to individual (organism) and then to ensemble (culture), for technical individuals do not reproduce as organisms do. Crucial, then, for coming to terms with technical evolution is not to mistake the function of the technical individual. We must not assume that humans should play that role, for in effect, we then begin to collapse the distinction between human and machine, entering into a war over which will play the role of technical individual. The facts of technical evolution suggest to Simondon that, rather than impose rectilinear progress on technicity, humans should insert themselves into the true tendency of technical evolution, which is nonlinear and discontinuous, by situating themselves alongside technical individuals, and thereby participating equally in the relation between technical elements and technical ensembles. The result would be, if we paint it in utopian hues, technical ensembles and fields of rationality that assume and prolong equality-in-difference, between humans and between humans and machines. This is what machines might do with us.

As Combes points out, that terms such as "should" and "true" arise in Simondon presents a certain risk, as does his use of reason, universality, and progress: we must be careful not to read such terms in an entirely normative fashion, as if Simondon were saying, "Because reality is this way, you have to align yourself with it."[34] Simply put, if you're not becoming, you're wrong. Like Combes, I feel that such a normative reading of Simondon ultimately is not justified by his project as a whole, but it is crucial to signal such a risk, because other commentators have opted for the normative reading: having-to-become.[35] In any event, the way in which humans are to insert themselves into the nonlinear evolution of technical being entails a movement that might well be described as neoteny.

In the pages on "minority" and "majority" in *Du mode d'existence des objets techniques*, for instance, Simondon presents a kaleidoscopic contrast between something like the juvenility or immaturity of human beings, on the one hand, and their maturity and reason, on the other. Here, too, there are risks of a normative reading, not least because, in delineating juvenility, Simondon folds peasants and other historical instances of inferiorized social strata into the mix. His aim, of course, is not to repeat the inferiorization of certain social groups or to categorize them as juvenile or immature. Nor is his goal simply to appropriate or recuperate them, even though his sympathies usually seem to align with the minority. Rather, as with Deleuze and Guattari's notion of the minor, Simondon strives to trace out countertendencies (and potentially counteractualizations) to the "major" tendency in which technological evolution has been mapped onto human evolution, making linear progress appear natural, reasonable, and inevitable. In effect, like Deleuze and Guattari, Simondon's politics of technology tends to become localized around a becoming-minor within the majority, though in the specific instance of modern technical ensembles. Yet, contrary to popular interpretations of it, such an approach does not rule out minoritarian opposition to the majority. Rather, it does not reify opposition by grounding such opposition in dualist and substantialist metaphysics, which tend to work by identifying minorities and making them assume their oppositional destiny as established by the metaphysician of history in substantialist terms.

In any event, humans' becoming-minor vis-à-vis technical individuals in Simondon hinges on a kind of neoteny of the human being, in which humans "return" to a moment that might be described as historically prior to their usurpation of the role of technical individual, to a more juvenile relation to technology that entails a genuine reckoning with technical elements as technical values that are autonomous of other concerns, such as economic value. With this "rediscovery" of the essence of technicity, humans will no longer strive to play the role of technical individual, or to play the role of servant or master to machines. The new role for humans might be described as technician, physician, or diplomat vis-à-vis machines, which implies the discovery of new kinds of technical ensembles for working with machines, closer to laboratories, hospitals, and embassies than to factories. Indeed, in an era when communications technologies have enlarged the politics of what counts as work, as a complement to Combes's emphasis on the political usefulness of seeing in the perspective of factory workers a form of counterknowledge, we should add the perspectives of these other workers-with-machines. At the same time, we should resist the temptation to signal one specific perspective or figure to bear the historical or evolutionary burden of transformation, which would transform the politics of knowledge into the politics of militant redemption.

Simondon's description may indeed verge on the utopian and redemptive, if it is not qualified in relation to politics, and if we lose the concern for specificity and thus techniques and apparatuses. In effect, the role of the human in Simondon is reminiscent of what Foucault called the "specific intellectual" in contrast to the universal intellectual.[36] It implies a politics in which one's technical role or technical value is not beside the point, but is instead the point of departure, what brings you to the threshold. Unlike Foucault, however, Simondon does not contrast the specific intellectual with the universal. This is because, in Simondon, as human beings rediscover technical value, they also discover technical equality, and in effect, technical universality. There are now, however, multiple universes, because as Simondon embarks on his inquiry into the technical essence of the human, he discovers the "place" of the human, that is, the relation of the human in the universe. The essence of the human lies not in natural right, natural sovereignty, or even communicative reason. It lies in technical equality, which can now be glossed as the relation between efficiency and finality, between efficient causality and final causality, which is also the "neutral point" of the human where its technical eventfulness transforms the power to technically affect and to be technically affected by universes of value. As Simondon concludes in his essay on the limits of human progress: "The questions of the limits of human progress cannot be posed without that of the limits of thought, because it is thought that appears as the principal depository for evolutionary potential in the human species."[37]

Notes

On Being and the Status of the One: From the Relativity of the Real to the Reality of Relation

1. Trans.: I here translate *il y a* as "givenness," in keeping with *il y a* as a gloss on *es gibt*, frequently rendered as "givenness."

2. A compound of *hylê* (matter) and *morphê* (form), this term designates the theory, Aristotelian in origin, explaining the formation of the individual through the association of form and matter; form, which is ideal (*form* may also be translated by the Greek term *eidos*), is impressed upon matter, which is conceived of as passive.

3. From a lexical point of view, this opposition between *à travers* ("through" or "by way of") and *à partir de* ("from" or "on the basis of") expresses the great distance separating processual thought from foundational thought. We find the same distance once again in the plane of language, for instance between French and more processual languages like English. Not having turns of phrase and modes of conjugation indicating processuality (like the English form *-ing* that indicates an action "in the process" of happening) available to him in his language, Simondon is to some extent constrained, in order to introduce dynamism into thought, to invent a style. For all its subtlety, this style is nonetheless tangible, relying in large part on a specific usage of punctuation: it is thus not rare to see deployed, in a phrase composed of brief propositions connected with semicolons, all the phases of a movement of being or of an emotion (see, e.g., his fine pages on anxiety in *IPC*, 111–114; *IL*, 255–257).

4. Such is at least the translation proposed by Jean Beaufret for Fragment II of the Poem of Parmenides: "*to gar auto noein estin te kai einai*"; Jean Beaufret, *Parménide: Le Poème* (Paris: Presses Universitaires de France, 1996), 78–79. To facilitate reading, I have systematically translated Greek terms in Latin characters, including those in citations from Simondon's works.

5. We could point to any number of other points in common between these two antisubstantialist philosophies, beyond all the critiques of Spinoza within the work of Simondon for not having accorded to the individual its true reality.

6. Trans.: Combes uses the term "squaring" (*au carré*) in the mathematical sense of raising to another power.

7. Anne Fagot-Largeault, "L'individuation en biologie," in *Gilbert Simondon: Une pensée de l'individuation et de la technique* (Bibliothèque du Collège international de philosophie, Paris: Albin Michel, 1994), 21.

8. It suffices to evoke the "multitude of corpuscular realities on which technicians and researchers act in order to impose accelerations, concentrations, measurable and predictable deviations" (*IG*, 256; *IL*, 554).

9. One may be surprised by Simondon's choice of physics for the paradigm for the study of the processes of constitution of beings—a study, he says, that has yet to be carried out. By virtue of a scientific gaze that is by definition deemed objective, physics seems able to concern itself only with constituted beings. Yet, if it is true that physics has not posed the problem of individuation as has Simondon, it has, from the early twentieth century, integrated an awareness of constituting its objects into its procedures, or at least an awareness of modifying them by means of the act of scientific observation itself. As such, it has necessarily been led to question itself about what a physical individual exactly is, and to make pronouncements on the reality of ontological consistency.

10. Gilbert Hottois is the author of the first introduction to the work of Simondon, *Simondon et la philosophie de la "culture technique"* (Brussels: Éd. De Boeck, 1993), 39.

11. Trans.: Combes cites this edition and these pages of Marx's *Capital*: *Le Capital*, Book I (Paris: Presses Universitaires de France, 1993), 121–125; 166–175. To her citations, I add citations from this English edition: Karl Marx, *Capital*, volume 1: *The Process of Capitalist Production*, trans. Samuel Moore and Edward Aveling (New York: International Publishers, 1987).

12. Marx, *Le Capital*, 123; *Capital*, 107–108.

13. Marx, *Le Capital*, 173; *Capital*, 161–162.

14. Following this ontogenetic perspective, the yellow color of sulfur must itself be explained as appearing in the course of the individuation that is operated within the superfused solution. Although Simondon does not speak of the formation of the color of sulfur, it seems important to signal that his description makes possible an ontogenesis of color, that is, an explication of the manner in which the yellow *of sulfur* is formed at the same time as the sulfur crystal; which is quite different from what a phenomenological description would give. In effect, phenomenology shares with the philosophy of individuation the rejection of the substantialist approach that believes itself capable of defining the object independently of the predicates that can be attributed to it; countering Descartes, it will say, for instance, that one cannot make yellow a predicate of the substance "wax," that yellow is the yellow *of the wax* and the wax itself is nothing other than its yellow. Renaud Barbaras sums up

it quite well when he writes that what Descartes could not admit was that "the identity of the object is constituted straight from sensible qualities" (in *La perception*, Paris: Hatier, 1994, 24). But this phenomenological approach, in which the object is transitive to its sensible qualities, is still distant from Simondon's approach, in which the object is a *transductive* being: we might sum up what separates Simondon from phenomenology (despite his indebtedness to it, which he indicates by dedicating *L'individu et sa genèse physico-biologique* "to the memory of Maurice Merleau-Ponty") by saying that it is not enough, in his view, to pay close attention to the movement of appearing and to identify an object with the appearing of its being, which assumes that a perceiving subject is given; our thinking still needs to go deeper into systems in formation, or, as he writes in the context of his description of the formation of a clay brick, "we would need to be able to enter into the mold with the clay" (*MEOT*, 243), which would mean, in this instance, entering into the U-tube with the supermelted sulfur.

15. Linking together already individuated terms is what characterizes a *relationship*. The difference between relation (*relation*) and relationship (*rapport*), to which Simondon gives consistency, comes fully into its own in the "plane" of psychosocial reality, as we will see in the next chapter.

16. This appears on page 41 of André Kaan's translation of Hegel, *Principles of the Philosophy of the Right* (Paris: Gallimard, 1949/1963).

17. A term formed from the Greek *thanatos* that designates the god of death.

The Transindividual Relation

1. The notion of disparation occurs frequently in Simondon, designating a tension, an incompatibility between two elements of a situation, which only a new individuation can resolve by giving birth to a new level of reality. Vision, for instance, is described by Simondon as the resolution of a disparation between the image perceived by the left eye and the image perceived by the right eye. These two disparate two-dimensional images call forth a three-dimensional dimension as the only way to unify them.

2. Some recent studies in psychology also make apparent, although from another point of view, that the "self" is larger than the individuated being. Thus, in *The Interpersonal World of the Infant* (New York: Basic Books, 1985), Daniel Stern focuses on the progressive emergence of "senses of self" owing to which the infant, the baby, and the child enter into relation with their environment, showing that, before the constitution of the individual "self," the little human does not fuse with the outside but progressively constitutes diverse modalities of the self. Irreducible to "stages" of development, these senses of self bear witness to the existence of a well-informed affective life, that is, absolutely not chaotic and yet impersonal.

3. Beyond the frank recognition of our ignorance with respect to knowing how far the transformation induced by such an experience can go. Thus, after having affirmed that anxiety truly seems to remain in a state that cannot lead to a new individuation, Simondon complicates it in this manner: "However, we cannot be absolutely certain on this point: this transformation of the being of the subject toward which anxiety tends is perhaps possible in some rare cases" (*IPC*, 114; *IL*, 257).

4. For Simondon, all psychosocial individuation, insofar as its elements are necessarily already individuated beings, supposes a relative disindividuation of individuals. In such disindividuation, the nonindividuated potential contained in each of them is liberated, making itself available for a subsequent individuation.

5. "Before" this disindividuating relation, the individual indeed has a relationship to itself but only as a series of images and functions. One may well object that, "in the absence" of any encounter with another subject, a being can feel itself to be a subject within anxiety as a disindividuating relation to itself. It is true that anxiety, as an experience of preindividuality, is not an *individual* experience but already *subjective*. Yet, to the extent that the subject pushes to resolve within its individuality all the preindividual submerging it, we cannot say that it accepts itself as subject: anxiety is instead the experience in which a subject, *at the same time* that it discovers in itself a dimension irreducible to simple constituted individuality (precisely a "subjective" dimension), pushes itself to resorb that dimension within its individual being.

6. Trans.: The passage appears in italics, not capitals, in *IL*.

7. Gilles Deleuze, *Foucault*, trans. Seán Hand (Minneapolis: University of Minnesota Press, 1988), 97; French edition: *Foucault* (Paris: Éd. De Minuit, 1986), 104.

8. Deleuze, *Foucault*, 118; French edition: *Foucault*, 126. In this passage from his work on Michel Foucault, summing up in his own words some pages from *L'individu et sa genèse physico-biologique* (258–265 in the older edition), Deleuze relies on Simondon's renewal of the relationship between inside and outside in the domain of the living in order to propose a model of the topological folding of thought, which he sees at work in Foucault.

9. The point here is not to characterize so-called primitive societies in opposition to advanced civilizations. Although Simondon seems to go in this direction when he opposes closed communities to open societies (see, e.g., *IPC*, 275; *IL*, 519), we must not forget that this opposition is not historical for him but conceptual, and in fact, any "social group is a mix of community and society" (*IPC*, 265; *IL*, 513): thus, in any society, primary sociality and transindividual potential are superimposed on each other.

10. If the human species is not distinguished from other species by a difference in essence, we can ask ourselves to what extent it is still legitimate to speak of species. Simondon retains this notion, not in the Aristotelian sense of common genus and specific differences, but as applying to an ensemble of *behaviors* that determine

thresholds as a function of which we can distinguish, within living beings, groups of individuals whose behavior is similar due to identical conditions of individuation.

11. Recall that the Greek term *apeiron* is usually translated as the adjective *indetermined*.

12. This paradoxical relationship between intimacy and the common will be dealt with in greater detail in the "scholium" following this chapter.

13. See, e.g., *IPC*, 184; *IL*, 297: "The contract does not found a group, nor the statuary reality of an already existing group."

14. This is why the presentation proposed by Gilbert Hottois in his work *Simondon et la philosophie de la "culture technique"* seems to me quite debatable. Rather than taking into account Simondon's critique of anthropology, Hottois presents his philosophy as *juxtaposing* "an ontology of the becoming of being, a philosophy of nature . . ., a philosophy of technics. . ., a philosophical anthropology" (Hottois, *Simondon*, 8; see also p. 10), and understands his humanism (to which he dedicates an entire chapter) as concerned with a "coevolution of man and technics" (ibid., 13), without ever saying what exactly "human" means here.

15. This is notably the thesis developed by Bernard Stiegler, drawing on the works of Lacan on the mirror stage and on the work of Derrida, in the first two volumes of his work *La technique et le temps* (Paris: Galilée, 1994, 1996), whose third volume (forthcoming) is supposed to be dedicated to Simondon. I return to Stiegler's thesis in the fourth chapter, "Between Technical Culture and Revolution in Action."

16. Toni Negri, *Exil* (Paris: Editions Mille et Une Nuits, 1998), 12.

Scholium: The Intimacy of the Common

1. Gabriel Tarde, *Les lois de l'imitation* (Paris: Kimé, 1993), 47; cited in the introduction to this work by Bruno Karsenti, who remarks: "Through an entirely paradoxical reversal, Tarde thus situates imitation as the source of invention" (ibid., xviii).

2. These two expressions appear in Tarde, *L'opinion et la foule* (Paris: Presses Universitaires de France, 1989), 33, 34.

3. *Bulletin de la société française de philosophie*, vol. 52, 182.

4. Ibid., 188.

5. Ibid., 184.

Between Technical Culture and Revolution in Action

1. Simondon's "naturalism" does not in any way adopt the traditional opposition between nature and technics, for, as we have seen in the previous chapter, nature designates the share of *apeiron* or the preindividual reserve present in each of us.

2. "This study is animated by the intention of raising consciousness about the meaning of technical objects" (*MEOT*, 9).

3. This expression crops up so often in *MEOT* that I will not cite all the instances. It will have to suffice to signal these particular instances: 155, 157, 176, 188, 213–214, 230.

4. We read, for instance, that the notion of finality applied to becoming of the human in its relation to the world is inadequate, "because we can actually find restrained finalities . . . but there is not a single and superior end that we can super-impose upon every aspect of evolution in order to coordinate them, and give an account of their orientation through study of an end superior to all the particular ends" (*MEOT*, 156).

5. This "normativity extending well beyond [technical being]" and imposing itself on communities is also evoked in one of the supplementary chapters of *IPC*, on pages 264 to 267, which appear in the *IL* edition on pages 513–515.

6. Trans.: The term used in Hottois is "reliance," which may connote "dependency" as well as "linking" or "binding." Because, as Combes shows, Hottois tends to force relation into a function of bringing what has been separated back together, and thus a sort of religious function, I have consistently translated it as "rebinding."

7. See, e.g., page 87 of Hottois, *Simondon*, where Simondon's philosophy is presented in terms of optimism toward *legein*.

8. Ibid., 58.

9. Ibid., 111.

10. Thus, in the last four pages of *L'individu et sa genèse physico-biologique*, Simondon adds the following expressions: "Consciousness of the sense of transfer that the individual has as an individual" (*IG*, 244; *IL*, 332), "their amplificatory power" (ibid.), "provisional as a discontinuous phase of transfer" (*IG*, 245; *IL*, 333), "in abandoning its role of transfer" (*IG*, 247; *IL*, 335), and finally "the individual, amplificatory transfer arising from Nature" (ibid.).

11. "The technical object is valid or invalid according to internal characteristics that translate the schematism inherent in the effort by which it is constituted. . . . The adoption or refusal of a technical object by a society signifies nothing for or against the validity of this object" (*IPC*, 264; *IL*, 513).

12. At the time of writing, the first two volumes of *La technique et le temps* have appeared in print: *La faute d'Épiméthée* (vol. 1, 1994) and *Disorientation* (vol. 2, 1996). Stiegler announced that the third volume would be devoted to Simondon, but because it was not yet published at the time of writing this account, my reading naturally is limited to the first two volumes; because my critique deals with the postulates for Stiegler's interpretation, the ground for my critique should stand as such.

[Trans.: in subsequent notes, I cite from the English translation of these two volumes: *Time and Technics*, vol. 1: *The Fault of Epimetheus*, trans. Richard Beardsworth and George Collins (Stanford: Stanford University Press, 1998) and *Time and Technics*, vol. 2: *Disorientation*, trans. Stephen Barker (Stanford: Stanford University Press, 2009).]

13. *Time and Technics*, vol. 1: *The Fault of Epimetheus*, 18; *La technique et le temps, tome 1: La faute d'Épiméthée*, 31.

14. *Time and Technics*, vol. 2: *Disorientation*, 2; *La technique et le temps, tome 2: Disorientation*, 10.

15. Ibid.

16. *Time and Technics*, vol. 2: *Disorientation*, 8; *La technique et le temps, tome 2: Disorientation*, 16. See too p. 10 (p. 18) where Nietzsche is designated as "the most profound thinker of power, that is to say of technics."

17. *Time and Technics*, vol. 2: *Disorientation*, 10; *La technique et le temps, tome 2: Disorientation*, 18.

18. *Time and Technics*, vol. 2: *Disorientation*, 2; *La technique et le temps, tome 2: Disorientation*, 10.

19. *Time and Technics*, vol. 2: *Disorientation*, 7; *La technique et le temps, tome 2: Disorientation*, 15.

20. This is the question posed by Giorgio Agamben in *Homo Sacer: Le pouvoir souverain et la vie nue* (Paris: Seuil, 1997), 19. [Trans.: I have not used the phrasing from the English translation here because it introduces additional concepts (*zoé*) not used by Combes. See Giorgio Agamben, *Homo Sacer: Sovereign Power and Bare Life*, trans. Daniel Heller-Roazen (Stanford: Stanford University Press, 1998), 11.]

21. A comment by Marx in the margins of *L'idéologie allemande*, Karl Marx and Friedrich Engels (Paris: Éditions socials, 1974), 90, n. 1.

22. Edward P. Thompson, *The Making of the English Working Class* (London: Penguin Books, 1991), 604. Pages 569 to 659 in particular are devoted to the English Luddite movement. [Trans.: Combes cites from the French translation: Edward P. Thompson, *La formation de la classe ouvière anglaise* (Paris: Gallimard/Le Seuil, 1988), 499.]

23. Thompson, *The Making of the English Working Class*, 599; *La formation de la classe ouvière anglaise*, 495.

24. Thompson, *The Making of the English Working Class*, 581; *La formation de la classe ouvière anglaise*, 480.

25. Thompson, *The Making of the English Working Class*, 603; *La formation de la classe ouvière anglaise*, 498.

26. It is striking to see to what degree, in the conclusion of *MEOT*, when he describes the technical activity supposed to lead beyond work, Simondon anticipates the mutations that have occurred in the organization of work since the 1980s. In a sense, any post-Fordist entrepreneurial organization relies on integration, within the work situation, of qualities of invention, cooperation, etc., required by technical ensembles. The entire question lies in knowing if the capitalist enterprise can *support* technical activity or if technical activity is not what exposes the enterprise to the danger of implosion.

Afterword: Humans and Machines

1. Ian Hacking, "Canguilhem amid the Cyborgs," *Economy and Society* 27: 2 (1998): 202–216.

2. Donna Haraway, "A Cyborg Manifesto: Science, Technology, and Socialist-Feminism in the Late Twentieth Century," in *Simians, Cyborgs, and Women* (New York: Routledge, 1991), 152.

3. I am thinking here of the work of Peter Sloterdijk. Even in his early work, in *Thinker on Stage: Nietzsche's Materialism* (trans. Jamie Owen Daniel; Minneapolis: University of Minnesota Press, 1989), Sloterdijk challenges us to think ethics in terms of cybernetics: "If ethics is cybernetics, we can understand why it pursues no objectives but, rather, processes breakdowns" (81). While his work does indeed effectively pose a challenge to subject-centered analyses of modernity, cybernetics becomes such an all-encompassing structuration of the contemporary world (a massive modernity thesis, as it were) that difference itself—ontological, social, political—drops out of his model, much as Simondon warns in the context of Wiener's cybernetics, and we are left with the lone figure of the navigator or helmsman, the cybernaut.

4. In fact, in beginning with the cyborg model, I am in effect reprising Simondon's point of departure in *Du mode d'existence des objets techniques*, which begins with a polemic against a popular understanding of machines as becoming autonomous and taking over the world from humans.

5. See Henning Schmidgen, "Thinking Technological and Biological Beings: Gilbert Simondon's Philosophy of Machines," paper presented at the Annual Meeting of the Society for Social Studies of Science (4S) in Paris, August 27, 2004. Online: http://www.csi.ensmp.fr/WebCSI/4S/download_paper/download_paper.php?paper=schmidgen.pdf.

6. Georges Canguilhem, "Machine and Organism," trans. Mark Cohen and Randall Cherry, in *Incorporations*, ed. by Jonathan Crary and Sanford Kwinter (New York: Zone Books, 1992). See also Hacking, "Canguilhem amid the Cyborgs," 203.

7. Schmidgen, "Thinking Technological and Biological Beings," 2.

8. Alberto Toscano, "La disparation," *Multitudes* 18 (2004). This is true provided we keep in mind that Simondon explicitly distances himself from thermodynamic energetics in favor of a sort of informational energetics, and that he rejects information theory.

9. One effect of Simondon's procedure of analogy is that it makes visible (and operative) an analogy between substantialism, dialectics, cybernetics, and hylomorphism. Here, too, he does not collapse the difference between these approaches but attends to their tendency to remain content with parity, which amounts to a general indifference to disparity.

10. Didier Debaise, "Qu'est-ce qu'une pensée relationnelle?" *Multitudes* 18 (2004): 15–23.

11. I am borrowing "concern" from Isabelle Stengers, which she explains nicely in the essay "The Cosmopolitical Proposal," in *Making Things Public*, ed. Bruno Latour and Peter Weibel (Cambridge, MA: MIT Press, 2005). Stengers's notion of a "concern" stems from Deleuze's notion of a "problem."

12. In a workshop on Simondon held at the Sense Lab in Montreal, in an unpublished presentation, Brian Massumi suggested the expressions "neutral point" and "remarkable points" for understanding crystallization in Simondon.

13. See the section entitled "Absolute Origins of a Technical Lineage," in *Du mode d'existence des objets techniques*, especially pages 40–43.

14. Toscano, "La disparation," 2.

15. The language of "part" and "partage" in Simondon implies both partition or distribution and sharing. This is difficult to render in English, and translations of Bataille and Rancière tend to highlight the problem, for *la part maudite* becomes the "accursed share," and *le partage du sensible* becomes the "distribution of the sensible."

16. Debaise, "Qu'est-ce qu'une pensée relationnelle?"

17. Giorgio Agamben provides a nice account of how Foucault's notion of *dispositif* glosses Kuhn's paradigm in *The Signature of All Things: On Method* (New York: Zone Books, 2009), 11–16.

18. Simondon often uses the term *chargé*, which means at once "charged," in the sense of electrically charged, and "burdened."

19. In her introduction, Combes also suggests that we can read Simondon's work through the lens of topology, even though he in fact rejected topology, or at least, as Combes points out, a certain understanding of it. See this volume, 42.

20. See Michel Foucault, "Truth and Power," in *Power/Knowledge*, ed. Colin Gordon (New York: Harverster Press, 1980), 109–110.

21. Combes discusses the accusations of objectivism leveled at Simondon by his peers in the context of a paper delivered in 1960; see this volume, 53–55.

22. Combes discusses this problem at great length in in this volume in "The Transindividual Relation," in which she shows that the subjective transindividual and the objective transindividual are two facets of the same reality.

23. I am coining the term "aesthetic equality" to summarize Rancière's approach, building on his own summation of what is at stake in the aesthetic regime: "the aesthetic regime is the implementation of a certain equality," in "Janus-Face of Politicized Art: Jacques Rancière in Interview with Gabriel Rockhill," in *The Politics of Aesthetics: The Distribution of the Sensible* (London: Continuum, 2004), 52.

24. Simondon refers us to phyla and families, which is also a way of avoiding the Aristotelian impasse of species and genera.

25. Paul Dumouchel provides a nice overview of the stakes in Simondon's discussion of engines, in "Simondon's Plea for a Philosophy of Technology," in *Technology and Politics of Knowledge* (Indianapolis: Indiana University Press, 1995), 225–271.

26. Martin Heidegger, "The Question Concerning Technology," in *The Question Concerning Technology and Other Essays*, trans. William Lovitt (New York: Harper & Row, 1977), 3–35.

27. Steven Shaviro, "Cosmopolitics," from *The Pinocchio Theory*, http://www.shaviro.com/Blog/?p=401.

28. Isabelle Stengers, "A Constructivist Reading of *Process and Reality*," *Theory, Culture, and Society* 25 (4) (2008): 92.

29. Michael Foucault, "The Subject and Power," afterword to *Michel Foucault: Beyond Structuralism and Hermeneutics* (Chicago: University of Chicago Press, 1982).

30. Simondon does indeed use the term "feedback," but because of his resistance to cybernetics, and because I see something very different at work in his philosophy than in theories of autopoiesis, I have put "feedback" in scare quotes.

31. See, e.g., Stephen Jay Gould and Richard C. Lewontin, "The Spandrels of San Marco and the Panglossian Paradigm: A Critique of the Adaptationist Programme," *Proceedings of the Royal Society of London B* 205 (1979): 581–598. For a cogent recent critique of adaptationism, see Jerry Fodor and Massimo Piatelli-Palmarini, *What Darwin Got Wrong* (New York: Farrar, Strauss & Giroux, 2010).

32. Combes also evokes this aspect of Spinozean bodies in explaining Simondon. See this volume, 9; 30–31.

33. Stephen Jay Gould, *Ontogeny and Phylogeny* (Cambridge, MA: Harvard University Press, 1977).

34. Combes, too, addresses the potential normativity of Simondon in her critique of Hottois's study that construes his philosophy in terms of a "having-to-become." See this volume, 63.

35. This notion of "having-to-become" is also where evolutionary theory can be forced into the sort of theory of sovereignty found in the work of Carl Schmitt. In "Criminalization: Carl Schmitt and Walter Benjamin's Concept of Criminal Politics," *Journal of European Studies* 39, no. 3 (2009), Udi Greenberg provides a nice summary of Schmitt's approach: "In his famous critique of liberalism and the parliamentary system, Schmitt argued that the two confused politics with the logic of commerce, and sought to subordinate the former to the latter. . . . The central position occupied in the liberal system by free and open discussion represented its naïve aspiration to transcend the political grouping of friend and enemy, which Schmitt's eyes was the basic principle of human organization" (308). As Giorgio Agamben has argued, especially in *State of Exception*, trans. Kevin Attel (Chicago: University of Chicago Press, 2005), such an understanding of sovereignty is not grounded in social contract but rather in violence. Combes reminds us that, while we must accept the challenge of thinking the collective beyond the logic of social contract, we then confront the risk of taking certain forms of violence as normative, as Schmitt does. A similar risk attends the notion of having-to-become insofar as it implies that the violence implicit in evolutionary becoming is somehow natural, and thus justifiable or even normative.

36. Michel Foucault and Gilles Deleuze, "Intellectuals and Power," in *Language, Counter-Memory, Practice* (Ithaca, NY: Cornell University Press, 1977), 205–217.

37. Gilbert Simondon, "Les limites du progrès humain," in *Gilbert Simondon: Une pensée de l'individuation et de la technique* (1959; reprinted, Paris: Albin Michel, 1994), 275.